MW00962079

SHAKING THE RATTLE; HEALING THE TRAUMA OF COLONIZATION

Barbara-Helen Hill

© 2017 Barbara-Helen Hill
All rights reserved.

ISBN: 1546643354
ISBN 13: 9781546643357

DEDICATION 1

In the first edition of Shaking the Rattle Healing the Trauma of Colonization, I wrote the dedication to my children and eventually my grandchildren and the generations to come. I was looking at future generations because that is what we all should do. To me that means being mindful of how we use and not overuse: to be aware that the food we have is much better grown in healthy soil: the air we breathe is much better if we have trees to filter the toxic gases that are exuded from factories and automobiles etc.

DEDICATION 2

I dedicate this book to all who are helping to heal the people from the trauma caused by remnants of colonialism, such as residential schools.

TABLE OF CONTENTS

ACKNOWLEDGEMENTS

With gratitude I acknowledge the Creator, my family, and friends for their support. Thank you to all those mentioned in the first edition. To Bob Antone, Diane Hill, and Donna Jenson for teaching me how to feel, teaching me the names of those feelings and that it was okay to feel them. To Rick Puteran for teaching me Reality Therapy and that I have the right to meet my needs. Thank you to Mary Lee and the pioneers of Adult Children of Alcoholics; Jane who taught about trauma in families; and all the men and women that I have met through NANACOA and other conferences. I have learned so much from all of you.

A big thank you to Marlena Dolan, Greg Young-Ing, Beth Cuthand, Jeannette Armstrong, and all the students and staff of Theytus Books and the En'owkin Centre who helped with the production of the first edition. I am forever grateful to all the people that I have met and spoken with throughout the years.

In this second edition I want to add that I especially thank the teachers in my life; Paula Sevestre for helping me with the second edition; Don Lynch for the line editing and being the 'comma man'; Linda Metcalf, Ann Mullen, and all the people in my writing circles for their encouragement anyone else that I reached out to.

INTRODUCTION

The first edition of this book was started in the late 80's when I, jokingly, left a message on my answering machine: "I can't come to the phone right now; I'm writing a book and when I'm finished this chapter I'll call you back." Someone took me seriously and passed the word along to a book publisher in the United States who encouraged me to write this book. From the initial thoughts about writing the book, there were many editions, edits before it finally went to press in 1995. Now it is 2017 and it is time for the second edition.

At the time, not only had I been made aware AA and AL-Anon but a group called Adult Children of Alcoholics. Finally, there was a place where I could make sense of my life and what I'd learned, experienced, and grown up with in my home as a child. Not all adults who attended these meetings with me had parents who were alcoholics. What I began to see was that there were other things that could be traumatic to a child. There would be too many groups if we listed all the traumas so I and others attended the Adult Children of Alcoholics.

There were local meetings and then there were conferences. The National Association for Children of Alcoholics USA was formed in February 1983. At one such conference in Orlando Florida there were a group of people from various Native/Indigenous communities that got together and decided to form the National Association of Native American Children of Alcoholics; the first meeting was in Minnesota. These conferences, both NACOA and NANACAO, have been very powerful healing places for starting and continuing to heal trauma from residential schools.

At that time there was also the "Inner Child" which is the child-like aspect of our selves. It is everything that we have learned and experienced before puberty. From Wikipedia, "The Twelve-step program recovery movement considers healing the inner child to be one of the essential stages in recovery from addiction, abuse, trauma, or post-traumatic stress disorder. In the 1970s, the inner child concept emerged alongside the clinical concept of codependency (first called Adult Children of Alcoholics Syndrome). These topics remain very active today. Carl Jung is often referenced as the originator of the concept in his Divine Child archetype. Emmet Fox called it the 'Wonder Child' Charles Whitfield dubbed it the "Child Within".

What I have found is that the complex information on healing techniques boils down to a simple idea for me – the healing of emotional pain. My first few counselling sessions were with Bob Antone and Diane Hill of Tribal Sovereignty Associates. From my first session, I was able to reach and heal some of my most disturbing emotions. I openly cried in front of others which I don't remember ever doing before. They didn't shame me; they didn't make fun of me; and most importantly, they didn't tell me to "shut up."

This book is based on experiences in my personal healing and the training that I have received through counselling. It is also based on composites of characters made up from clients and some experiences that they had and shared with me. Counselling and working through my traumas was a learning process for me. It was ironic and synchronistic that every time I experienced healing in one of my traumas, I was counselling someone else in something similar.

The basis of this book and my recovery is spiritual. I lost two important people in my life to alcoholism related diseases in 1981. That's when I began to attend AA, Al-Anon, and then Adult Children of

Alcoholics. I was given the gift of spirituality by removing the blocks to wellness through the emotional healing. The emotional healing gave me a powerful gift. Removing the painful subconscious memories and feelings, I also was able to take in more of life and connect to the spiritual world – all of the world. The wholeness of me, mental, physical, emotional, and spiritual me could then connect to others, as well as the natural world. I was no longer isolating myself.

I've structured the book to best relate my experiences using fiction and nonfiction. I have incorporated poems, short stories, and narrative essays to provide the reader with a comfortable learning format.

This book is not designed as a linear thinking self-help book. It is by no means a technical, theoretical book. I have written this book the way that I teach – plain, simple, and with gentleness. We do not get hurt in a straight line or in steps and so I haven't written this that way. This book is a "dipper." You don't have to read it from cover to cover to obtain the information or understand the concepts. This book can be opened anywhere; at the beginning of any story, poem or informational piece. Dip in and something will be there for you.

We open with a poem by my daughter. I share this poem with you and we begin our journey – one step at a time. For never again will I or we be "shut up."

Silent Tears

> They are so muffled and quiet
> But yet they are so very loud
> I am afraid someone will hear me
> "Shut-up, before I give you something to cry about."
> It hurts so much
> Please, let me scream!
> Hold me, and help me get it out.
> I'm older now.
> No one to tell me to shut-up

My tears are silent
Why can't I scream?
It hurts so much. Please, let me scream!
Hold me, and help me get it out.
by Monica L. Stevens October 30, 1989

PROLOGUE

I heard a girl recently say that her grandmother was taken to residential school because there wasn't enough money or food for her and her younger sister in a family of sixteen. She never talked about residential school, the girl went on to say, until her grandmother was close to the end of her time. When she finally did speak, she said, "The residential schools took away our self-confidence. It took away our dignity, and it took away our life, our heart, and for some, our soul."

I didn't go to residential school but I was in a public school on the territory, or what some call a reservation, when the residential schools were still in operation. The message was the same as in the residential schools. We understood that the man/father was the head of the household. We had to go to church and we were never taught the language. My father told me, when I asked about learning Mohawk, that he never taught us that because he didn't want us to be beaten.

I had little or no self-confidence, and I was always afraid of offending. I was afraid of making a mistake, doing wrong or even doing harm. I wasn't taught to harm but I wasn't taught that any of my words or actions might cause unintentional harm. I also had buried my heart and I imagined a world where everyone loved everyone, where there was no fighting, where there was no anger, no fear, no hurts, and where there was no drinking.

Residential school, although good for some, was detrimental to so many others. It clearly was intended to eradicate any and all culture, language, traditions, and teachings from all Indian children. In some cases, it worked so it was good or successful for the churches and government. It's undeniable that is was good for some children who received an education and a place to live where they had food, even if it was spoiled and/or wormy.

Residential school divided our community but it didn't conquer it. There were some children who were sent to residential school because their families had no way of supporting them, with little money and not enough food. Some were taken away and sent to residential school because of misbehaviours and, for them, it was a punishment –a kind of reform school. I guess you could say that it was a reform school from its inception because they wanted to reform our people from "savages and pagans to good little educated Christian Children."

The teachings and treatment in those schools changed the children and when they returned, there was some anger at those who didn't go. There was also some arrogance in the ideas of we are better than you; we have an education; we are better than you because we know God; and you are just pagans because you don't go to church. They started to believe the school's rhetoric and started to put down their former friends and relatives.

The people left at home carried on with their lives and their ceremonies. The differences were obvious. The families in some cases were torn apart. But we weren't conquered. We are still here although much has changed. There are many churches and many that attend. There are still the same number of longhouses but they have had to be enlarged because many more are attending the ceremonies. And there has been a renewal of the languages with three emersion schools being built and adult language programs are well attended.

Many people don't understand why the Residential Schools were established and until recently it wasn't discussed among the non-Native population. I've done some research and the best way to understand is to look at the list from the 1000 Conversations:

"Brief History of Residential Schools"
In the 1870's, the Government of Canada partnered with Anglican, Catholic, United, and Presbyterian churches to establish and operate boarding and residential schools for Aboriginal (First Nations, Inuit, and Métis) children.

The intent of the Residential School System was to educate, assimilate, and integrate Aboriginal people into Canadian society. In the words of one government official, it was a system designed "to kill the Indian in the child."

Attendance at residential schools was mandatory for Aboriginal children across Canada, and failure to send children to residential school often resulted in the punishment of parents, including imprisonment.

The federal government and churches operated over 130 residential schools across Canada. The number of active schools peaked in 1931 at 80. The last federally-administered residential school closed in 1996.

The federal government currently recognizes that 132 federally-supported residential schools existed across Canada. This number does not recognize those residential schools that were administered by provincial/territorial governments and churches.

Over 150,000 children (some as young as 4 years old) attended federally-administered residential schools.

It is estimated that there are approximately 80,000 Residential School Survivors alive today.

If you want to know more then you can find the information at:
http://1000conversations.ca/?page_id=48

Maggie

> Her long silver hair tied in a black ribbon shone in the
> lamp light as she danced
> floating on moccasins of soft, beaded doeskin follow-
> ing in footsteps of generations past
> on glistening hardwood floors polished from dance
> steps

with years of resonating song and laughter in
Longhouse walls.
Silver broaches glint in sunlight
that pours through cracked windows as I watch
her lightness in movement
gentle as butterfly wings.
Turtle rattles shake; water drums beat out the rhythm
heart beats
songs that
sing babies to sleep give way to love
with rabbit dance
stick dance
laughter echoes
on the warm air.
Day turns to evening and stars glisten
Creator and Spirits guide our way
as language, song, dance, and harmony fills the room
I join her in movement
the song, the laughter, thanksgiving
feasting and sharing joy and laughter wrinkles
disappear
deep enough at one moment to hold water
then smoothed with a smile
eyes sparkle
deep within
the heart beats in time with the drum
love emanates out of the pores
as sweat beads and dissipates
in ceremonies that bar no one
because all must be able to celebrate
the Creator's gifts.
Barbara-Helen Hill 1995

1

COLONIZATION: EFFECTS ON NATIVE PEOPLES

The Europeans came to the Americas filled with fear. They were running from fear and from their oppressors who had taken over their lives and their lands. In coming to the Americas, they only had to fear the unknown. They came and brought with them their views and teachings. They brought their fear of the devil and the teaching that their God was a punishing God. They came with beliefs that women and children were to be owned as chattels. They came with fear of their own teachings, of their God, and especially of the devil that they understood to live in the dark – the dark forests. They were escaping from the Renaissance period in Europe where they were under religious persecution, political degradation, and darkness. It is said that the only good that came out of the Renaissance period was the art.

The Indigenous people of the Americas were living free, well-balanced lives. They were spiritual people at one with the Creator and all that the Creator had given them here on their Mother Earth. They did have their trials and they did war against another nation for their hunting space and/or areas for villages. But as children they learned to be grateful for all that was received. The animals taught them to share by giving their lives to provide food and clothing. They wasted nothing. Sharing was a common practice with one another and whoever came to the villages. They gave thanks for and used everything.

To the European, in their fear, the forest was uncivilized and only the children of the devil would live there. Indigenous people learned that there was nothing to fear amid the trees or animals or plants living in those dark forests. Europeans became afraid of the people they called the "Devil's Children/Savages." What do you do with that which you fear? You do everything that you can to overcome and overpower that fear. The Europeans used many methods to conquer and "civilize" the "Devil's children." Today we refer to those efforts with words like integration, acculturation, assimilation, racism, and genocide.

Today in reading the *Indian Act* or the "Historical Development of the Indian Act" produced by Indian and Northern Affairs in 1978, one would get the idea that this Act was for the good and betterment of the people. The government and the military conceived, drafted, and passed the *Indian Act* without any consultation or consent from Natives. The original version of the *Act* first came into effect in 1876 under a government that believed that Indians had no special rights as the original occupants of the land. The government thought that the original inhabitants should be eliminated as distinct peoples and assimilated as soon as possible into the mainstream of Canadian society.

The *Indian Act* has been used to deny Natives the right to vote, to strip women of their status as "Indian" and prevent them and their children from living in their communities. The Act required "Indians" to ask for permission to leave their reserves, to declare that wills written by "Indians" are invalid, to declare that a federal government official be the chairperson for band council meetings, and to ban sacred ceremonies which are a central part of their lives.

The *Indian Act* maintains the paternalistic attitude and colonialist relationship to this day. Through this "authority" the federal government retains ultimate jurisdiction over reserve lands: Bands must get the Minister of Indian Affairs' permission to develop resources on reserve, while, the Minister can grant outside parties' permission to exploit resources on reserve. Any person who writes a will must have the will authorized and administered by an Indian Affairs official. These are just a few examples of how the *Indian Act* worked. The *Indian Act* has undergone minor revisions in 1886, 1906, 1927, 1985, and 1988, as well as a major revision in 1951. However, its basic principle remains the same –to assimilate, integrate, or annihilate.

In reality, by the time of the American Revolution, the Haudenosaunee (people of the longhouse) had over 150 years of intermittent warfare. From 1784–1838 most of the Haudenosaunee territory was taken under fraudulent treaty or treaties obtained by means of coercion.

> *"The Haudenosaunee," composed originally of five nations and later six are more commonly known as the Iroquois Confederacy, and are an ancient people of North America. Our tradition states that our people originated in the northeastern woodlands of North America. There are no stories within the tradition concerning migration across frozen lands to the area we occupy. We have been, and continue to be, the original inhabitants of these lands. There was a time when our lands were torn by conflict and death and where certain individuals attempted to establish themselves as the rulers of the people through exploitation and repression. We emerged from those times to establish a strong democratic and spiritual way of life. The confederate state of the Haudenosaunee became the embodiment of democratic principles which continue to guide our peoples today. The Haudenosaunee became the first 'United Nations' established on a firm foundation of peace, harmony and respect." (Basic Call to Consciousness 1978:1)*

The many years of disease and warfare were one cause of people's spirits becoming broken. More had taken to drinking or had sunk into states of apathy. Our people were split. Some were forced to flee to Oklahoma, Kansas, and Wisconsin. Others fled to the promised lands in what is now called Canada.

The treaties and promises of the governments of the United States and Canada were ploys to assimilate and integrate the Indigenous people into mainstream society. The first attempts were by the missionaries and educators. Boarding schools and churches were ways of taking people from their spiritual base. When that was not moving quickly enough, they pursued more drastic measures.

> *"In 1892, New York State forcibly placed an illegal government in the Mohawk territory of Akwasasne and passed laws restricting the traditional governments in the Native territories. Canada did the same.*
>
> *In 1924, both the United States and Canada passed citizenship laws which allegedly imposed citizenship upon Indigenous people. The Haudenosaunee or Six Nations/ Iroquois Confederacy, notified both countries that they would remain citizens of their own country. Canada responded by sending the military to Grand River country and forcibly expelling the traditional government.*
>
> *In 1934 the United States passed the Indian Reorganization Act which was designed to destroy the traditional governments and impose colonial elective band councils." (Basic Call to Consciousness 1978:3)*

These acts carried out by the United States and Canadian governments had the effect of dividing and conquering the people. The assault on the Confederacy Council in 1924 and the forced implementation of the elective system, led to further split within the community at Six Nations.

These acts attacked the spiritual core of the people and reverberated outwards. They reacted with response patterns which surfaced as feelings of powerlessness and hopelessness. These feelings started within individuals and spread outwardly to family, community, and eventually nations. The tactics of both the United States and Canadian governments, of signing treaties and promising gifts or deals, were ploys to rid themselves of their guilty consciences for their persistent efforts of destruction.

> *"Haudenosaunee has – over a period of 375 years met every definition of an oppressed nation. It has been subjected to raids of extermination from France, England, and the United States. Its people have been driven from their lands, impoverished, and persecuted for their Haudenosaunee customs. It has been the victim of fraudulent dealings from three European governments which have openly expressed the goal of extermination of the Haudenosaunee. Our children have been taught to despise their ancestors, their culture, their religion, and their traditional economy. Recently it has been a government sponsored fad to have bi-lingual/bi-cultural programs in the schools. These programs are not a sincere effort to revitalize the Haudenosaunee, but exist as integrationist ploys to imply 'acceptance' from the dominant culture." (Basic Call to Consciousness: page 70)*

The Haudenosaunee succumbed to apathy and the response patterns of hopelessness and powerlessness. Conditions that surface in the communities today such as suicide, alcoholism, family breakdown, inhalant abuse, and other forms of abuse are the symptoms of the much deeper underlying problems.

The history of our families and past generations has led to the dysfunction of today's society. The abuse of alcohol, drugs, food, sex, gambling, work, and relationships are all cover-ups for the pain we carry – generations of pain.

The needs of Native people for safety, belonging, and feeling good about themselves are denied because of the negative stereotypes that are prevalent. These negative images are perpetuated in history books, movies, religious paintings of "savages and pagans", and the racist remarks – both obvious and elusive. These messages impact our thinking and self-concept as well as our identity as Native people. We question our original forms of existence, <u>and the entire form of existence enters a state of 'anomie.'</u>

This is described in *The Power Within People* by Antone, Hill and Myers: "Anomie denotes a people's loss of faith and belief in their own institutions, values, and existence."

The people in our territories have come to the attitude of "what's the use," even in the battles between families and neighbours.

The people who want to live the traditional ways are subjected to internal oppression within the communities. They are judged, labeled, and condemned because they don't "measure up." Many times, because of choosing to go to the Longhouse, I was called a pagan. Others were labeled "slow learners" in school because they did not learn the English language as quickly as their peers. Choosing not to follow the ways of the government-controlled band council, but choosing to follow the Great Law, has labeled many as rebels and trouble makers.

During initial contact with the Europeans, the Indigenous people developed a pattern for survival. These response patterns varied. People converted to western religions, cooperated with the authorities, and/or rebelled. Whatever the family chose to do was the family "theme," and that choice was passed down from generation to generation to meet their needs for survival.

Looking back a few generations, I saw that my family had chosen to adopt the western religion and cooperate with the authorities. I came to this realization and rebelled. I left the western religious beliefs, and returned to my traditional Longhouse beliefs. I was rebelling against the oppressive conditions of the church and the family theme. I was not about to stay in that family pattern. I was breaking out even if it meant I had to quit school, drink, and run away from home to regain the power and hope that was lost.

Family themes are not constructed with the idea of freedom. It was based on the beliefs that were originally created as a result of the negative messages from their oppressors. It came from a belief that the Europeans were more powerful. The Europeans came with the belief that everything was chattel, property to be purchased, stolen, or owned, including the women and the children.

These beliefs have intermingled with ours for generations and now we have sexist battles within the Haudenosaunee territory. These are confusing issues for the children in families where they learn about the matrilineal society and yet see male dominance and abuse. The warfare, the alcohol, the apathy, and the generations of intimidation led the Natives to believe that they had no rights. Being born into that kind of family theme, a person is unlikely to meet their psychological needs and this results in the impediment of the individual's natural human development.

Many traumas that Native people experience originate from "Ethnostress." Ethnostress is a term coined by Diane Hill, Bob Antone and Mike Myers back in the early eighties.

> *"Ethnostress occurs when the cultural beliefs or joyful identity of a people are disrupted. It is the negative experience they feel when interacting with members of different cultural groups and themselves. The stress within the individual centres around the self-image and sense of place in the world. Beginning on an individual basis, the effects of the "Ethnostress" phenomena are analyzed and then applied to the collective groups of family, community, and nation." (The Power Within People, page 7)*

The trauma of "churchianity" and government control resulted in frozen groups of people without trust in themselves, let alone others. I use the word "churchianity" because it is not necessarily Christian teachings that are wrong, rather, the church's interpretation that has destroyed our people.

Ethnostress encompasses layers of pain that each individual carries on their back. It's like a heavy load that we carry from one generation to the next, and has the effect of leaving us feeling powerless and hopeless to do anything about our state of affairs. We are not the only ones to suffer Ethnostress. Every dominated and oppressed person in the world has experienced this trauma. I know of a strong Catholic woman who was beaten to force her to give up her French first language and is as traumatized as the children of residential schools. To renew the spirit and heal the communities, we must start on an individual basis to heal the self.

As a result, the term "internalized oppression" can best describe the communities' behavior. With internalized oppression, social pressure affects human thinking and feeling. The pressures, whether physical or psychological, work to restrict and limit an individual's spontaneity and freedom to think and feel. As the individual absorbs the thoughts and feelings projected upon him/her by the oppressive conditions, he/she in turn develops behavior patterns. The behavioral patterns are usually viewed as negative and distressful. These patterns stem from survival or defense mechanisms that were used in helping families cope. The patterns work to protect the individual while suppressing the human spirit.

Internalized oppression is operating in communities all across Indian country. The internal fighting, the racism, the prejudice – all the "isms" – are a result of internalized oppression. The Europeans inflicted pain on the Native people, and now they are projecting that pain onto each other. The result being spousal and child abuse, homophobia, and the conflicts between the traditional and elective systems.

The battles, the political oppression, the social oppression, the economic oppression are tools of genocide.

> "Genocide is alive and well in Haudenosaunee territory. Its technicians are in the capitals of Ottawa and Washington. Its agents control the schools, the churches and the neo-colonial elective system offices found in our territories. This oppression has taken its toll but the Haudenosaunee continues to meet its challenges." (Basic Call to Consciousness, page 71)

Further to that statement, is the fact that the patterns still persist in the communities that existed in the 1800s. There was alcoholism then, promoted by its easy availability, and there is alcoholism now. The schools were set up to divide and conquer. The Education Act of 1927, where Indian kids were forced into the white education system, successfully split the family and community members. These splits still persist in our communities today; as in the conflict of the traditional beliefs versus Christianity. This conflict still runs strong in the communities. It was originally started by the churches and the education system in the residential schools, to divide and conquer, and has all but succeeded. This division was instrumental in promoting internal racism that presently exists in the communities. Where once stood proud and honorable people, now stands beaten, fearful, and angry people.

We need to revitalize our social and political institutions. The removal of internal pain that we individually carry can accomplish this. Healing the generational pain and returning us to the healthy basis from which we came can return the people to their original state, prior to colonization. It starts with an individual that is tired of oppression, colonial domination, and confusion. It does not mean that we go back to living in longhouses; it means we bring the teachings into the present. It means that we start to walk the talk and we do that by listening to each other.

The Peacemaker's teachings spoke of not only the establishment of law and order but for the full establishment of peace. Peace was not just the simple absence of war, but the active striving of the people for the purpose of establishing universal justice.

The principles of law set forth by the Peacemaker sought to establish a peaceful society by eliminating the cause of conflict between individuals and groups. Listening to another person validates them, which in turn promotes healing of the pain instead of projecting it outwards in anger. The law was also based on a logic which looked to nature for its parameters. It is one of the few examples of "natural law."

If you observe natural law, you will find that everything has a purpose. View yourself as being part of a spider's web. There are plants, animals, insects, reptiles, amphibians, birds, and every species created, including humans, within this web. If you remove the human from the web, everything still goes on. Remove an insect, a plant, or even an animal, and the whole chain is disrupted. Only humans are expendable from the web, because they have no significant effect on the food chain.

Following the natural law and seeking to establish the peaceful society can be accomplished by eliminating the conflict inside. To successfully establish a peaceful society, one must heal first as an individual, then as a community. Individually, when we remove the pain that blocks our connection to the Creator, we reach for that love within and let it emanate out. We can co-exist as a community and as a nation. Without this connection, we will end up destroying the natural world.

This may sound like "pie in the sky philosophy," but I believe that by healing the individual we will be able to prevent the destruction of the food chain or the spider's web, because we will no longer need to destroy in our anger, greed, and fear.

Never Again

> Never again
> Will they take you from our land
> Will they cut your hair and douse your head
> to rid you of the bugs that only they could see
> Never again
> Will they strip you of your identity, make you one of
> them–
> Like all the rest
> And steal your humanity, Individuality
> Spirituality
> Never again

I say these words
I watch
As you cut your hair and douse your head in colours
To expel the internal creatures
That only you can see
To erase the pain and grief
That you carry for your parents, grandparents, and ancestors
The endless pain
Once more I hear the words Never Again
As I watch you walk away
To the cities and towns
To the bars and streets
Still carrying the pain
I yearn to bring you home and say Never Again
And yet, look, I am there
Beside you,
Within you, surrounding you, I am there
Haunting you, for I,
In my pain,
Did the same
As our grandmothers and grandfathers
Stood helplessly by
As you were taken
By their ways, their words,
Never again I say
As I walk away
No longer a child in their cities,
In their towns
Their words no longer control
Their liquor no longer runs in my veins
My blood flows red with my ancestors
Pumping, beating the drums of our songs.
Our hearts,

Our spirits
Now soar with eagles, ravens, hawks
And carry our prayers to the Creator
We will tell our children
And grandchildren for generations
How we have endured, survived and maintained
We say never again.
Barbara-Helen Hill 1995

2

RESIDENTIAL SCHOOLS: THE IMPACT AND GENERATIONAL UNWELLNESS IN NATIVE COMMUNITIES

In 1880, the Canadian government and the churches set up residential schools. The children were taken, literally stolen in some cases, and placed in these schools. In other areas, the Indian agents and the priests went in and told the parents that they had to put the children in those schools. Parents didn't understand the language much less the idea of the schools and watched helplessly as their children were taken away.

Among other things, nutrition was poor in these schools. Later, when the children returned home to their communities, they went back to the natural way of eating. In the 1950s, the residential school kids were still on a poor diet, but by this time, upon returning to their home communities, the diet awaiting them was also poor. Parents were working or on subsistence and by now were on westernized diets. Traditional food became a delicacy not a staple.

By 1995, children are on a strictly western diet. There are no more traditional foods except in a few strong traditional communities and that is mostly for ceremonial purposes. Wheat, sugar, yeast, and dairy products were not a part of our traditional diet. Therefore, the bannock was not and is not traditional food and neither are sugary deserts. It is no wonder that many Natives are finding themselves with a high rate of obesity, heart disease, diabetes, and other diseases. The body is now consuming foods that it does not recognize. Alcohol consumption causes numbing of emotional and mental pain. Many people with eating disorders are trying desperately to numb the pain. Is the pain yours? Are you carrying someone else's shame? Are you stuffing yourself with sugary, starchy foods to numb some pain? Do you need to release the pain, especially if it is not yours to carry? Lack of loving touch, emotional support, and just plain physical and emotional deprivation may cause eating disorders.

Our extended families have changed drastically with colonization. Many of our parents and grandparents were raised in boarding schools. They were not taught the natural parenting skills and therefore lacked those skills to love unconditionally, nurture, and listen, as the pre-residential school parents had. Those skills were omitted from their boarding school curriculum and, being away from their homes, they did not have the opportunity to learn from their parents.

In about 2013/14, I was fortunate to hear a talk given by John Moses. In his talk he shared that his father had been at what became known as the Mush Hole – a name given to the Mohawk Institute Residential School in Brantford Ontario, Canada. I'm privileged to be given the permission to print this letter and the letter from Indian Affairs requesting that Mr. Moses submit his recollections.

In 1965 a letter from Indian Affairs Branch, Department of Citizenship and Immigration signed by Mr. Jampolsky, Superintendent of Vocation Training and Special Services was sent to Mr. Russ Moses. In the letter he was requested to put some thoughts on paper about residential school for a meeting of the Residential School Principles in Elliot Lake in January of 1966.

Quoting from the letter:

> *"In order to bring as many viewpoints as possible to these deliberations, a selected number of Indians have been invited to submit their views and you are one of the persons who has been selected.*

We would be most grateful to you if you would put your thoughts regarding residential schools down on paper and send this to me by the end of December. Please feel free to express your views candidly. We want to benefit both from your experience and your insights and frankness will be appreciated."

There were, of course, the usual yuletide greetings and it closed with Mr. Jampolsky's signature.

The following are the words of Mr. Russ Moses in his reply to the Indian Affairs request.

"MOHAWK INSITITUTE – 1942-47

First, a bit of what it was like in the "good old days".

In August 1942, shortly before my 9ᵗʰ birthday a series of unfortunate family circumstances made it necessary that I along with my 7-year-old sister and older brother be placed in the Mohawk Institute at Brantford, Ontario.

Our home life prior to going to the "Mohawk" was considerably better than many of the other Indian children who were to be my friends in the following five years. At the "mushole" (this was the name applied to the school by the Indians for many years) I found to my surprise that one of the main tasks for a new arrival was to engage in physical combat with a series of opponents, that was done by the students, so that you know exactly where you stood in the social structure that existed.

The food at the Institute was disgraceful. The normal diet was as follows

Breakfast *– two slices of bread with either jam or honey as the dressing, oatmeal with worms or corn meal porridge was minimal in quantity and appalling in quality. The beverage consisted of skim milk and when one stops to consider that we were milking twenty to thirty head of pure bred Holstein*

*Cattle, it seems odd that we did not ever receive whole milk and in my five years at the Institute we **never** received butter once.*

This was very strange, for on entering the Institute our ration books for sugar and butter were turned in to the management – we never received sugar other than Christmas morning when we had a yearly feast of one shredded wheat with a sprinkling of brown sugar.

__Lunch__ – At this Institute this consisted of water as the beverage, if you were a senior boy or girl you received (Grade 7 or above) one and half slices of __dry__ bread and the main course consisted of "rotten soup" (local terminology) (i.e. scraps of beef, vegetables, some in a state of decay.) Desert would be restricted to nothing on some days and a type of tapioca pudding (fish eyes) or a crudely prepared custard, the taste of which I can taste to this day.

*Children under Grade V level received **one** slice of dry bread – incidentally we were not weight watchers.*

*__Supper__ – This consisted of two slices of bread and jam, fried potatoes, **NO MEAT**, a bun baked by the girls (common terminology – "horse buns") and every other night a piece of cake or possibly an apple in the summer months.*

The manner in which the food was prepared did not encourage overeating. The diet remained consistent, hunger was never absent. I would say here that 90% of the children were suffering from diet deficiency and this was evident by the number of boils, warts and general malaise that existed within the school population.

I have seen Indian children eating from the swill barrel, picking out soggy bits of food that was intended for the pigs.

At the "mushole" we had several hundred laying hens (white leghorn). We received a yearly ration of __one__ egg a piece – this was on Easter Sunday morning, the Easter Bunny apparently influenced this.

The whole milk was separated in the barn and the cream was then sold to the local dairy firm, "The Mohawk Creamery", which I believe is still in business. All eggs were sold as well as the chickens at the end of their laying life – we never had chicken – except on several occasions when we stole one or two and roasted them on a well concealed fire in the bush – half raw chicken is not too bad eating!

The policy of the Mohawk Institute was that both girls and boys would attend school for half days and work the other half. This was Monday to Friday inclusive. No school on Saturday but generally we worked.

The normal work method was that the children under V level worked in the market garden in which every type of vegetable was grown and in the main sold – the only vegetables which were stored for our use were potatoes, beans, turnips of the animal fodder variety. The work was supervised by white people who were employed by the Institute and beatings were administered at the slightest pretext. We were not treated as human beings we were the Indians who had to become shining examples of Anglican Christianity.

I have seen Indian children having their faces rubbed in human excrement, this was done by a gentleman who has now gone to his just reward.

The normal punishment for bed wetters (usually one of the smaller boys) was to have his face rubbed in his own urine.

The senior boys worked on the farm – and I mean worked, we were underfed, ill clad and out in all types of weather – there is certainly something to be said for Indian stamina. At harvest time, such as potato harvest, corn harvest for cattle fodder – we older boys would at times not attend school until well on into fall as we were needed to help with the harvest.

We arose at 6:00 a.m. each morning and went to the barn to do "chores". This included milking the cattle, feeding and then using curry comb and brush to keep them in good mental and physical condition.

After our usual sumptuous breakfast, we returned to the barn to do "second chores" 8:00 to 9:00 a.m. this included cleaning the stables, watering the young stock and getting hay down out of the mow, as well as carrying silage from the silo to the main barn.

We also had some forty to eight pigs depending on time of year – we never received pork or bacon of any kind except at Christmas when a single slice of pork along with mashed potatoes and gravy made up our Christmas dinner. A few rock candies with an orange and Christmas pudding which was referred to as "dog shit" made up our Christmas celebrations. The I.O.D.E. sent us books as gifts.

Religion was pumped into us at a fast rate, chapel every evening, church on Sundays (twice). For some years after leaving the Institute, I was under the impression that my tribal affiliation was Anglican rather than Delaware.

Our formal education was sadly neglected, when a child is tired, hungry, lice infested and treated as a sub-human, how in heavens name do you expect to make a decent citizen out of him or her, when the formal school curriculum is the most disregarded aspect of his whole background. I speak of lice; this was an accepted part of "being Indian" at the Mohawk – heads were shaved in late spring. We had no tooth brushes, no underwear was issued in the summer, no socks in the summer. Our clothing was a disgrace to this country. Our so called "Sunday Clothes" were cut down first world war army uniforms. Cold showers were provided summer and winter in which we were herded on mass by some of the bigger boys and if you did not keep under the shower you would be struck with a brass studded belt.

The soap for performing our ablutions was the green liquid variety which would just about take the hide off you.

Bullying by larger boys was terrible, younger boys were slaves to these fellows and were required to act as such – there were also cases of homosexual conduct, but this is not strange when you consider the boys were not even allowed to talk to the girls – even their own sisters, except for 15 minutes once a month when you met each other in the "visiting room" and you then spoke in hushed tones.

Any mail coming to any student or mail being sent was opened and read before ever getting to the addressee or to the Indian child – money was removed and held in "trust" for the child.

It was our practice at the "Mohawk" to go to begging at various homes throughout Brantford. There were certain homes that we knew that the people were good to us, we would rap on the door and our question was "Anything extra", whereupon if we were lucky, we could be rewarded with scraps from the household – survival of the fittest.

Many children tried to run away from the Institute and nearly all were caught and brought back to face the music – we had a form of running the gauntlet in which the offender had to go through the line, that is on his hands and knees, through widespread legs of all the boys and he would be struck with any-thing that was at hand – all this done under the fatherly super-vision of the boys' master. I have seen boys after going through a line of fifty to seventy boys lay cry8ng in the most abject human misery and pain with not a soul to care – __the dignity of man__!!

As I sit writing this paper, things that have been dormant in my mind for years come to the fore – we will sing Hymn No. 128!!

This situation divides the shame amongst the Churches, the Indian Affairs Branch and the Canadian public.

I could write on and on and some day I will tell of how things used to be – sadness, pain and misery were my legacy as an Indian.

The staff at the Mohawk lived very well, separate dining room where they were waited on by our Indian girls – the food I am told, was excellent.

When I was asked to do this paper I had some misgivings, for if I were to be honest, I must tell of things as they were and really this is not my story but yours.

There were and are some decent honourable people employed by the residential schools, but they were not sufficiently in number to change things

SUGGESTED IMPROVEMENTS FOR RESIDENTIAL SCHOOLS

1. *Religion should not be the basic curriculum, therefore, it is my feeling that non-denominational residential schools should be established (dreamer).*

2. *More people of Indian ancestry should be encouraged to work in residential schools as they have a much better understanding of the Indian "personality" and would also be more apt to be trusted and respected by the students.*

3. *Indian residential schools should be integrated – the residential school should be a "home" rather than an Institute.*

4. *Salaries paid to the staff members should be on a par with industries – otherwise you tend to attract only social misfits and religious zealots.*

5. *The Indian Students should have a certain amount of work (physical) to do – overwork is no good and no work is even worse. I believe that a limited amount of work gives responsibility to the individual and helps him or her to develop a well-balanced personality.*

6. *Parents of Indian children should be made to contribute to the financial upkeep of their children – I realize that this would be difficult, but it at least bears looking into.*

7. *Each child should be given individual attention – get o know him or her – encourage leadership, this could be accomplished by giving awards for certain achievements*

8. *Last, but most important, solicit ideas from the students, we adults do not know the answers.*

SUMMATION – *The years that an Indian spends in an Indian residential school has a very great deal to do with his or her future outlook on life and in my own case it showed me that Indians are "different", simply because you made us different and so gentlemen I say to you, take pains in molding, not the Indian of tomorrow, but the Canadian citizen of tomorrow. FOR "As ye sow, so shall ye reap".*

It is dated 28/12/65 and the name Russell Moses is typed, and although not clear, I'm thinking it says Student of Mohawk Institute

The document was sent to me by John Moses, son of Russ Moses, and because it is in picture form and not able to be incorporated in that format, I am grateful to John for the permission and opportunity to include this "retyped" letter in this book.

Boarding school residents know what it is like to be hungry. They know what it is to eat spoiled food. Often, they ate leftovers as punishment. Boys and young men need more food than do girls and young women. Often they received food equally proportioned or, as punishment, less than their female counterparts. Our relatives often went hungry. Part of that deprivation resulted in the obsession with food some carry to this day. Those raised in boarding schools may have an extreme need to fill the cupboards and refrigerator with food before they are even low. The obsession with food is part of an eating disorder.

Often in recovery from any addiction, people may find themselves getting panicky when they are running low on money. My first thoughts are, "Do I have enough money for food?" This, I realize, is part of the disease. Obsessive, compulsive thoughts about food often plague us even into our recovery. We may be on an abstinent meal plan and doing quite well, but the thoughts are there.

According to Mike Myers, coauthor of *The Power Within People*: "If there is no loving touch we will find it by using comfort foods. This results in eating disorders. We transfer eating disorders along the lineage memory."

Myers describes lineage memory as follows: "at the time of conception, the grandmothers gather around and instill the memories critical to our life. Our gifts and our DNA are stored inside the mitoneuron in the cell. These memories and gifts are a natural part of our lives." When our grandmother, for example, was in the boarding school and went hungry she stored that memory at the cell level because it was not critical to survival. The hunger is passed on in the lineage cell memory to us as grandchildren and we have a vulnerability towards obsession for food and especially the comfort foods. These are not conscious feelings. Anxiety, fear, anger, loneliness, hurt, any feeling, even happiness can trigger the compulsion to eat.

Anorexia is an eating disorder which is really a form of slow suicide. Starvation. Sexual abuse is commonly at the bottom of eating disorders. This sexual abuse often is so buried that there is no conscious memory of it. Or the parents have been sexually abused and have not resolved that abuse. They try to protect and are in extreme control of the child. The child fights for survival of her/his own identity. She/he can live with parents being in control by going back to being a little child. The child is emaciated, zoned out, and disconnected so she/he can cope with the family. This results in a self-destructive pattern that causes refusal to eat. By deliberately choosing not to eat, the child has some kind of control of her/his life since they feel that one way of feeling in control is through food: "If I don't eat, I will disappear and so will the pain. If I don't eat, I will lose my shape, and I will no longer look attractive to men, and they will not hurt me anymore. If I don't eat, I will not look like an adult; I will continue to be Mommy and Daddy's little girl."

Bulimia is binging or gorging on food and then purging by shoving your fingers down your throat forcing yourself to vomit, or abusing laxatives to empty the bowels. Natural laxatives are no different from other over the counter laxatives as they still produce the same effect. Continuous self-induced vomiting can lead to vomiting without the hand down the throat. It can become automatic. Bulimia has serious side effects. Bulimics very often have rotting teeth and hair that becomes brittle and lifeless.

The human body is very sensitive, and the repulsion of necessary food materials affects the function of the body. The addictive nature of bulimia causes the body to expel food automatically, as the disease progresses. The body no longer functions without laxatives. It will mean, in recovery, to retrain the body to eliminate on its own. It will mean that the vomiting will become easier, and often it can be such an addiction that in recovery you know that you are getting better when you only stick your head in the toilet five times instead of twenty or thirty.

This disease is about power. The person suffering with the disease is trying to regain power and control of her/his life. The individual may not have been sexually abused in their recollection but often they have.

> "The anorexic and bulimic often become promiscuous because of the unresolved issues of their parents. Their parents may have been sexually abused and have pushed the issue away from their conscious memory. They become rigid and controlling, and their children become rebellious and tend to act out the dysfunction through sexual promiscuity. This promotes shame and the bulimia becomes more evident and pronounced because the child needs the parents' approval." (Martha Peirce of Penn Rose Associates, Hagersville, Ontario)

It is a family disease. The parents and the rest of the family need just as much or more counselling and help as the anorexic or bulimic. Inside every anorexic and bulimic is a young child saying, "I need to be me." Eating disorders are about parents needing the child to stay dependent. In one way or another the person is fighting for her/his life, and control of her/his life.

Regaining individual power is an important step in recovery. In counselling, the person regains power a little at a time. Allowing the person to choose their appointment times, letting them choose the length of time and how often they attend counselling sessions, helps them regain their own power. Giving them the information that they need and allowing them to disclose a little at a time builds their trust. In all eating disorder cases, individuals have been robbed of their power through the abusive lives they have lived.

Food addiction is common in society today just like alcohol and sometimes even more so. Foods such as sugar and refined carbohydrates ferment in the stomach. This causes a numbing of feelings as do alcohol and other drugs. To not feel painful emotions, people will overdose on chocolate, ice cream, pastries, French fries, potato chips, or anything that makes them forget. They often are not even aware that they are pushing away the pain that is subconsciously trying to come to the surface. Then the shame comes up, so they purge or eat to cover the shame.

Eating disorders, for a long time, have not been recognized as a life-threatening disease. Doctors and healthcare people often put people on diets, recommend prescriptions, and other forms of "helping" the person when they need to be confronted and assisted in their recovery. There are more eating disorder patients now being recognized by clinicians than ever before. It has taken many years for people to get the help they need.

Looking at our eating habits takes tremendous strength and often requires support. It takes courage to look at what we crave, what we eat too much of, and how often. We need to have a dietician or someone familiar with eating plans help us set up a healthy way of eating. If we continue to eat foods that our bodies cannot identify or digest properly, what then are we doing to that wonderful gift that the Creator gave?

"If we eat like them we go crazy like them." Khatsalano said this to his people about eating the diet of the Europeans.

Khatsalano was wise in this statement. If we continue to poison our bodies, we will end up leaving a legacy of ill health for the generations to come.

Very often when people become ill with diseases uncommon to them, it is because of their diet. Many Native people, when tested for food allergies (usually as the last resort), have been found to be allergic to wheat, sugar, yeast and dairy products. Often children suffering from chronic ear infections have recovered almost immediately when they remove dairy products from the diet. I know for my own recovery – allergic to wheat – it causes bloating and often arthritic symptoms in my body. And if I choose to remain free from dairy products, I have very little sinus problems.

Before the Europeans came here to North America, Native people in different parts of the country ate differently. The Native people on the west coast ate from the sea. Iroquois ate mainly soups and vegetables and occasionally meat. People in the north had a totally different diet. They ate a lot of meat but not many vegetables or grains. People ate from the land, foods natural to their areas.

Our bodies are not able to digest properly and assimilate nutrients from foods in westernized diets. We did not have them naturally in our diets. We had corn and other grains. Maple syrup, honey and fruits sweetened the food, and no cows were available until colonization.

> "When you eat something you shouldn't, your body becomes confused and anxious. If the body cannot express itself, it becomes toxic." (Lee Maracle in a talk at En'owkin School of Writing and Fine Art, Penticton, BC)

In other words, we are poisoning our bodies and there are physical symptoms caused by these food allergies. Skin rashes, extreme

amounts of gas, sleepiness at the end of a meal, bloating, water reten-
tion, just to name a few.

People today are walking around eating from fast-food restaurants and not knowing what is in these foods. They are stuffing
themselves with things that may be toxic to their bodies. Just eating
them may be toxic to your body, and then on top of that, add the
chemicals and preservatives. The mega-buck corporations that run
McDonald's and all the fast food restaurants are putting chemicals
in animals to make them produce bigger, faster, and meatier animals. The faster and bigger the animals grow the more meat they
can sell. These chemicals are going into the food – the dairy products and the meats that we are eating. In turn they go into our bodies. The chemicals that produce fatter animals remain in the foods
when cooked. We are not able to maintain a body that is at its natural
weight. Children are overweight. Diet pills, diet centres, diet foods,
and other means of weight loss are also a big money making deal
for the same corporations. The money makers get you fat with the
chemicals in the foods, and then tell you that it is better to be thin in
their advertisements. The corporations then offer the diet pills and
diet centres to enable you to be thin. It is a corporate world that is
controlling our lives and our lack of health.

For many of you with an eating disorder you might want to trace
your history. Were any of your relatives in a boarding school? Did any
of them have to go hungry for any reason? Boarding schools were not
the only cause for hunger. There were wars, and the depression, pris-
oner of war camps, famine, diseases etc. that caused our relatives to
go hungry. We must remember that there are few full-blood Natives
and we need to look at the lineage memory in all the generations. If
we ignore a part of our heritage, we are ignoring a valuable tool to
help the next seven generations to wellness.

Another point about the boarding or residential schools is that
often the children lined up for their daily dose of cod liver oil and
castor oil. Castor oil, as you may or may not know, is a laxative. One
of the symptoms of our unhealthy lifestyles is constipation. It is a sign

of holding on to pain, memories, trauma etc. Any child who is put through trauma often becomes constipated. As an adult, new trauma or re-stimulated childhood trauma can cause constipation.

A child, ripped from its home and forced to live and attend school in a residential setting, often finds there is no loving touch. They find no familiar parental teachings and natural foods. Often there was physical and sexual abuse. I would assume that there would be constipation. Often it was a policy of the school, that once a week at least (or more often), they force-fed castor oil "for their own good." I wonder whether, within the lineage memory, there is also the need for laxatives. If a person growing up in the boarding/residential school is unable to have a healthy bowel movement without laxatives during childhood and still needs them regularly during adulthood, you could have a case of bulimia. Is the bulimia also travelling on our lineage memory trails? Are we suffering physical pain and emotional pain due to the eating disorders set up in the residential schools and, other traumas?

> *"The Iroquois left the Mohawk valley in 1794 in front of a massive famine. From 1514 - 1780 we lost 90% of our populations to diseases and we started to adopt to build up our population. In the Eighteen Hundreds the first epidemic of measles and smallpox combination ran through our villages. In 1850 a second epidemic came through–it was tuberculosis. From 1920 through 1935 another TB epidemic went through our villages."* (Mike Myers, Co-Author of the Power Within People – A Community Organization Perspective)

With this history, we know that many Iroquois went hungry. Knowing this history, we can see that it is possible that the memory of that hunger runs in our blood. We might look at how it is causing us to have eating disorders. Lineage memory is another tool to use in seeking help for eating disorders that we may have, and how we can go about healing them.

As recovering compulsive overeaters, people have a fixed, focal point of reference. Abstinence is the most important thing in their lives without exception. This may sound like a strong statement, but food addiction and food diseases are life threatening. Many people have stated that it's easy for alcoholics; they don't have to drink again, one day at a time. People have to eat, and it is difficult to eat only what is necessary for your life. Abstinence is a guide to recovery. Without abstinence we remain in pain and denial. We cannot look at the cause of the pain that is enabling us to eat if we are numbed out on sugar, starch, and other addictive foods. We need to abstain to look within in an honest way. Honesty with self is the only way to recovery. There are many ways to break the cycle. Remain abstinent from your addictive and compulsive foods, work with the tools given either by a recovery program or group and/ or through a counsellor, and stay connected to the higher power of your choice.

Exercise plays an important part in recovery. A note needs to be made here. Exercise stimulates the heart muscle and tones the muscles but it needs to be done in moderation. A doctor needs to be consulted, and we need to be careful not to become addicted to the exercising. That can also be part of the disease and by that I mean that a person can start exercising and it will replace another addiction that they are trying to quit like addiction to alcohol, sugar, breads, etc.

All these suggestions are ways to stop the lineage memory of eating disorders for your grandchildren and theirs for the next seven generations. We need to start putting positive healthy memories in those genes and cells for the future.

Our lineage memory carries those memories of the boarding school abuses. Our lineage memories also carry the memories of the natural, loving way that our extended families were at one time. Confusing, to say the least, when we long for and crave loving touch, but instead we get abused physically, sexually, emotionally, mentally and spiritually by those we should trust.

Recovery from eating disorders means looking within again. It means finding the inner child and re-parenting. When I speak of the "Inner Child" I'm referring to your spirit, that childhood memory you have of yourself. Re-parenting means to give the inner child (self) the love and attention and support that was not received during childhood. It means really paying attention to yourself and listening to your intuition, hearing what your body is saying about what it wants, not just eating because you are driving by a fast food place. It means giving the child the affirmations and the attention needed by re-nurturing without the sweets and the fatty fast foods. It means empowering the child-self or spirit within to maintain a healthy lifestyle and re-educating the self and removing the toxic foods from the diet.

Not all people are allergic to the same foods. To be sure it means seeking professional help. Naturopaths are a good source of that help. The medical profession still has, in many areas, not come to the conclusion that food allergies can cause illness. Find someone to listen to you and validate you. This may mean seeking help to come to the realization that you are worth it. That may take some work in itself.

Helping a person with eating disorders is difficult. It means the person has to look within to find the inner child and to help counteract the beliefs that the child carries. That inner child has memories of child abuse of one form or another. It takes time to have that child feel good about himself or herself. It is also about power. A sexually-abused child has had his/her power taken away. To regain their power, they turn to the only power possible–the power over whether or not to eat and how much.

> *"From this day forward I will accept nothing less than absolutely everything."* (Paraphrased-The Reclaiming of Power, Harvey Jackins 1987(9))

I will do this for myself and for the generations to come. We have suffered enough. It is time that we reclaim what is rightfully ours.

Healthy eating is going back to our natural way of eating. What were the foods that your people ate generations ago? What kind of grains did they have?

We put our bodies to the test of eating what it does not recognize. It strains to try to digest what is naturally poison. What then stops us from changing that? How do we stop ourselves from saying that we deserve the best? What stops us from returning to the healthy eating that we once had? Only you can decide. It is your body and your life. You make the decisions for yourself, despite what you were told. The one thing that I must remember is that I also make the decisions for the next seven generations.

As a result of the rules and regulations in residential schools many children were given an inferior education and by that I have the belief that the teachings should be inclusive not just memorizing useless information. I've taken the liberty to enclose a list of intellectual boundary violations and intellectual abuse taken from the book *Finding Balance* by Terry Kellogg, and Marvel E. Harrison published in 1991 by Health Communications. I'm using it in reference to what has happened in residential schools both in the US and Canada.

Boundary Violations and Intellectual Abuse.
Being denied information, given misinformation, being told what to think, told what we really mean when we say what we mean, being spoken for, being made fun of, being ignored, not listened to, always having ideas altered or improved upon, being treated with cruel mind games, being called names like stupid or dummy, not being recognized for special learning problems, being tested in non-supportive ways, having excess pressure to perform for grades. Having failed in classes where the teacher has not taught in the style in which we can learn. Not being allowed to make mistakes, belittled for asking questions, being overly

focused on for intelligence and being smart, having our curiosity stifled, not being taught in the paths of our interests, not being supported for continuing education, having no right to privacy of thoughts, being raised in a limited environment with the absence of people who provided stimulation and show us how to find information.

3

ABUSE: THE LEGACY OF COLONIALISM

Abuse is defined as "an active and damaging intrusion beyond the physical, sexual, emotional, intellectual, or spiritual boundaries that define individuals."

Physical Abuse
Physical abuse means violation of physical integrity whether it is hitting, getting too close to a person, or touching without asking.

Emotional Abuse
Emotional abuse invades the emotional parameters. People suffer emotional abuse when their unique emotional truth is discounted or rejected when they are subjected to ridicule, to raging outpourings, or to judgmental and derogatory comments.

Emotional abuse also occurs when a person is repeatedly treated with silent withdrawal and lack of attention.

During intellectual abuse, the thinking process is disregarded, disrupted, or discouraged. For example, when people's ideas or thoughts are subjected to destructive criticism, when they are harshly judged or punished for errors in reasoning, when they are authoritatively and rigidly told how and what to think without room for creativity or error, they are being intellectually abused.

Religious Abuse

Religious abuse occurs when religious rules, teachings, or rituals are imposed without permission. Children who are forced to accept their parents' unwavering and stringent belief systems, while their own spiritual truth is undermined or discarded, are being subjected to religious abuse. So are communities that are forced to follow specific theological programs under threat of punishment.

Spiritual Abuse

Spiritual abuse is different from religious abuse. Spiritual abuse includes all the other forms of abuse and more. Anyone who is being violated in any way is also being spiritually abused. If we accept the possibility that our deepest roots are sacred and then abuse each other, we are violating a sacred law of the divine. We are told that God lives within each of us. If we recognize that we are each a miraculous, unique thread in the web of creation, then we are all parts of the universe or "all my relations." When we violate others, we are also committing an act against the very core of our own being, against the creative source of our existence.

When we abuse someone, we generate fear, anger, hopelessness, confusion, guilt, and shame. These wounded individuals become victims and are walking, wounded children inside angry, fear-riddled adults. They are men and women void of any connection to their source of creation, and as the loneliness deepens their victimhood strengthens. That is spiritual abuse, loss of connection to the Creator and the self.

> *"Where there is excessive use of alcohol and/or other forms of drugs there are other forms of abuse. Where there is manipulation and control by co-dependent family members there is abuse." (Grof 1993: 53)*

If the statement made by Christina Grof were to be believed, then we have had abuse in our lives for more than a few centuries.

Looking back to the Renaissance period and the fear that brought the Europeans here to North America and South America, it is very much in our lineage memory or collective consciousness.

Any person or group who has an opinion that they are "better than others" frequently inflict abuse such as physical, emotional, intellectual, sexual, religious, and spiritual on those they deem to be inferior.

Missionaries and traders were intent on conquering not only their own fear of the unknown and the people that they thought of as the children of the devil, but also the people they thought were lesser than themselves. They wanted to tame, control, and convert the "savages." They tried to force unfamiliar, unnatural social and religious attitudes and ideologies on the Indigenous people around the world and specifically here in North America. The people were removed from their spiritual roots and their sources of inner inspiration and sustenance as well as from their rich cultural reference points. They were alienated from sacred lands and meaningful relationships with the natural elements, one another, and, in some cases, their Creator.

In her book, <u>Children of Trauma,</u> Jane Middleton-Moz writes that "ethnic shame," "self-hatred" and "learned helplessness" result from discrimination against those who are identified as inferior. As a result of the discrimination of the whites against our ancestors, we now carry that in our lineage memory and act out on each other. Our addictions, compulsions, illnesses and behaviours or misbehaviours are a result of these traumas that have been handed down. From these traumas, we have a nation of co-dependents, addicts, and people with a disease called depression.

One of the most disturbing things about a diagnosis of depression is that many people expect medication to "cure it" and that isn't always the case. Many of the symptoms of depression are common everyday occurrences for some people. Depression symptoms can be found in pamphlets in your doctor's office, on the internet, and in books. Depression can often be related to feelings of powerlessness, helplessness, and unexpressed anger.

It is not necessary to think that if you have one or two of the symptoms that you may read about you are clinically depressed. Clinical depression is another matter altogether. Depression symptoms may be relieved or alleviated by the healing of the emotional pain. Depression that is not a chemical imbalance, I am told, is anger turned inward. Counselling can help to remove the anger towards self. Most often the anger towards self is not deserved and stems from that helpless or powerless feeling about things you cannot change. If the anger is with respect to the sexual abuse you may have suffered as a child or even later, isn't that anger better directed towards the abuser?

The abuser is the one the anger should be directed towards. This does not mean that you should seek revenge. This means that you heal the emotional pain, get help for the physical pain and the spiritual will come into balance.

There is help out there for those who were abused. We just need to look. We also need to speak out against the abuse. If one has been abused by an elder or a priest, a teacher, a member of the clergy or anyone in power that person needs to tell someone.

All old people are not elders. Some still need to do their own healing. We need to speak of this because many people are still looking outward for the answers and can be re-traumatized and abused. Some young women have complained that they are instructed to go to an elder, offer tobacco, and ask for help, but they end up feeling worse than before they went to see the elder. The elders may be taking advantage of the vulnerability of the young women and making advances towards them, or they may have been judged or and/or criticized. The young women, many times out of respect, let the elder have his way and walk away, after being touched or kissed, feeling shame. That shame does not belong to that woman. The elder has crossed a boundary and has violated a trust.

Now all the blame is not always just on the elder. Many times there are women out there who, due to their own issues, may find a great attraction in an "elder." They enjoy the prestige of being with an "elder."

They allow and even lead the man to believe that it is okay with all women. It is not okay with all women. Because some women in their own sickness "make it" with elders, does not mean that all women are like that. This causes the elder to have mixed feelings or mixed messages, and if he has not healed his own issues, he will think that it is okay to treat all women the same. Some elders make advances, touch in inappropriate places, try to kiss these young women who offer tobacco and other such things. This needs to stop.

The young women need to find elders that they feel safe with. Women attend sweats with women only; men with men. No mixed sweats. There are, to my understanding, only a few necessary sweats where men and women mix. That is a special sweat, and it is a healing sweat that is conducted by a man and woman together. Only go to sweats and ceremonies where you feel honored, where your boundaries are honored by yourself and others. Do not go if you feel uneasy. Do not mistreat yourself. There are enough people out there who abuse each other; you do not need to abuse yourself by going to places where you do not feel safe.

Men need to take care of themselves in their own way. They need to honour themselves as well as the little boy or spirit inside. Many times as children, the little boy has been abused and not just by other men. Men have been abused by women, and we tend to attract or be attracted to women who are similar to the abuser. Women do the same with men. Taking care to honour the child inside and only being around people that feel safe is the first step to recovery.

Telling a "safe someone" allows us to break the silence. One is only as sick as their secrets. One does not necessarily need to go to court and press charges when they tell about the abuse. We need healing to get to a safe place within. A court case could be traumatic for oneself and the inner child, sometimes it means more abuse. One needs to be strong and emotionally healed or healing to go through with it.

Because of the tyranny of one culture over another, many Native people are experiencing the traumas of addictions with the results being abuse. These include physical, mental, sexual, emotional, and spiritual abuse. These are symptoms of the historical abuses and the grief and loss that we are now experiencing from generations past in our Native North American communities.

All of the abuse and addiction that we are seeing in communities are symptoms of the underlying cause, the oppression and the stress of living in isolation on reservations or in Native communities within the larger non-Native communities. The stress within the individual centres around self-esteem and sense of place in the world. The basic spiritual needs are not met because of this pain or oppression.

Healing the spirit of the individual will eventually spread to healing the spirit of the family and this in turn will spread out into the communities, and so on, until eventually the nations will be the positive role models for the rest of the world. Does this seem like Utopia? Maybe in my generation it is.

Healing really does start from the individual. The healing of the spirit begins with the abstinence from the compulsion and the addiction. This comes from the healing of the pains from the past and healing of the inner child. These counselling opportunities help the person/client become responsible for their actions and their healing by helping them heal the pain without placing blame. The healing that takes place encompasses the mental and emotional health of the individual as well as providing an avenue for preventing further abuse to self and others.

4

THE SNOWY OWL

Emily perched herself upon a stool. Staring out her kitchen window, she had a good view of the lake and the apple trees that covered the land sloping down to the shore. On the marble counter top lay her journal, pen, and coffee cup. The ceramic ashtray held her smoldering cigarette. The Marlboro Menthol pack was tucked neatly in her shirt pocket with her lighter encased in delicate beadwork that her daughter had made for her.

Her gaze shifted to the lonely elm tree. With most of its branches missing, the tree stood naked in the middle of the yard. What was left of the branches reached out to caress the wind.

Dawn was breaking over the hills and in the dim light Emily saw the Snowy Owl. She watched as the owl settled on the tree top. Feathers fluffed and fell into place as the owl nestled on her perch. Emily watched the action of Miss Priss, as she called her, and let the trail of smoke drift up and out from her cigarette. "Where have you been?" she silently questioned. "Why are you here? What's your message?" Emily knew that if she waited long enough she would get the answers to her questions. She had many questions lately, but being a freelance writer, it was part of her job to ask questions. She looked over at her typewriter and wondered if the Owl could help her write her article.

"Questions!" Emily thought about the phone call yesterday from her sister Callie. She had been in so much pain yesterday, sobbing on the phone. "Why had God dealt her such a blow?" She was always a good kid. "Is the Owl bringing me more messages?"

Emily thought of her sister. Callie had married her school sweetheart. She had been in love with him since grade school, and they seemed to have been born for each other. Callie had called to say that Ron had kicked her out. He had just told her to leave and to take her damn brats with her. Emily recalled her conversation with Callie as she walked over to the fridge to put the breakfast food away.

"I never thought of myself as alone with children," Callie had said, "I just never thought of anything but being with Ron."

"So what happened?" Emily asked.

"So what do I do now?" she said as if she hadn't heard Emily. "I know that I have to pack and find a place to live. Oh God, what do I do?"

"Well, you can go to welfare. You can find a house—say why can't he leave? How come it's always the women and children who have to leave, and the goddamn man sits on his ass in the house?"

"I don't want the damned house Emily. I don't want it if it means a fight!"

"You can't just sit there and think of making everything nice for Ron. You have to think about the kids and yourself," Emily stated and asked again," And what happened anyway? How come he's kicking you out?"

"Oh, he said that I am spending too much time on myself and not enough time on the marriage. He said I need to make a choice. I either stay home and do what he says or I leave. So I left."

"Something doesn't sound right here? What does he mean stay home and do what he says?"

"You know, no more having the Tupperware parties. I made over seven thousand dollars last year selling Tupperware. No more self-development courses and going out with my friends. I went to those classes once a month, and the only friends I go out with are you and Mom. According to him, I can go to Mom's house or maybe your house occasionally. The rest of the time, I'm to go to work, and home."

"Well excuse me Hitler," Emily said.

"Oh, Em, what do I do?"

"Sounds to me like you decided to leave. So why are you asking, what do you do?"

"Well I know this is asking a lot, but, well can I move into your place? I don't have anywhere to go for now and you know what with prices being so high and everything?" She was almost whining.

"Here?"

"No, silly, here in town. Your place over on Bernard. It's empty isn't it?"

"I put it up for sale. The real estate agent is showing it tomorrow. Oh I guess, you can live in it until I sell it or till you get your own place. I'll charge you rent so you can get welfare. And don't forget to nail the bastard."

"Oh. Emily, I can't do that. I love him. I just can't do what he says, you know–stay home under his thumb. A few years ago I would have jumped... but not now."

Now Emily sat smoking her cigarette and gazing out over the lake, thinking. Callie had been right. A few years ago she did everything that Ron asked. All he had to do was snap his fingers and point to his cup. Callie would run over and fill Ron's cup with fresh coffee. Then she would empty his ashtray. Shit.

Emily ground out her cigarette forcefully, imagining that she had Ron's face in the ashtray. Her fingers pushed and twisted on the cigarette butt like she was pushing and twisting his eyes and facial hair. "What a pig, just like men," she thought. She wanted answers. "What had happened?" But she knew it was really none of her business. She wanted so badly to grab him and drag him out of the house, and let her sister and the kids live there.

The Snowy Owl perched on the treetop. Emily wondered what was happening to the world. Her own marriage had failed. Her daughter was off alone in New York, and she feared that she would not make a go of her relationship. Callie and her broken marriage. "Where does it end? What was going on? Why are people so cruel? How could Ron do that? It's almost Halloween and damn cold out. Callie and the kids don't need to be looking for their own place. What a jerk. I have a mind to call him and tell him exactly what I think of him." But her grandfather had told her long ago, "If you just sit and listen the answers will come."

Emily got up and started to clear the counter. It was almost time to get ready for work. She washed the breakfast dishes and made her way up the stairs to the loft. Being self-employed had its advantages. Today she could wear her sweats and slippers. She had no scheduled meetings with anyone.

Coming down to the kitchen a few minutes later to make fresh coffee, Emily glanced out the window and noticed Miss Priss was still there. She stepped close to the pane and looked at her. She felt herself being drawn into her big golden eyes. Deep into the soul of the bird. The deep silence frightened her.

She grabbed her coffee and went to the typewriter. "What was the heading for this story to be?" Since she was a successful freelance writer, she often had magazines calling her and asking for stories. Now they wanted a story on the effects of colonialism on the Indigenous peoples of South America. They didn't bother looking at the effects on the Indigenous people of Africa, China, or North America. They now wanted to look at the people of South America. "When would they learn that the effects are right here?"

Emily's typewriter hummed as her fingers fluttered over the keyboard. Six pages later she took a break and read what she had written. She sipped her coffee and read.

It seems that the "endangered species" here on earth are not the little creatures like the Snowy Owl, the grizzly bear, or even the fine plants in the rain forest. The most endangered species here on earth are the humans themselves. They are not "damaging" the earth as stated by all the conservationist magazines because the earth can cleanse herself with earthquakes, floods, hurricanes, and any natural storm that she wants. She is not dying–we are. "Very good," she thought, "just a little editing and I'll have a first paragraph."

The insatiable human need to control, to buy, to steal, to operate with anger and hatred is poisoning the insides of them. Poisons are flowing out in wars, crime, and all kinds of abuse.

Emily questioned whether she should write about the Band Council's decision to take a protected land piece and construct a gambling casino because it would bring in revenue. She thought that if she wrote about it, the story would be like other Native communities she heard about. Casinos brought in money but also brought in crime and an element of distrust. It increased the already growing factions in the communities and the accusations of nepotism, causing continuous fights of family against family. She wondered if these people were going to see that white man's ways were only going to destroy. She thought of how it even said in the Great Law that Whiteman's ways would destroy the people and their ways. Not that gambling was always wrong, but the greed was. Emily shook off the feeling of fear and continued writing.

The internalized pain that is projecting out at one another causes the mistrust and the gossip and the backstabbing in the communities. We need not judge whether we are of one race or another when we believe in the Creator. I want to believe that inside the elders of the longhouses, the sweat lodges, and the churches and synagogues, are the leaders who walk with love in their hearts and the concerns of the people in their minds. I do not want to believe that these elders, philosophers, teachers, and medicine people are walking around with hatred and fear inside. I see that the younger people have that hatred and fear, and I'm afraid that the elders do too.

She remembered the incident about her friend Gail. The speaker of the Longhouse questioned her about why she was there. He said there had been a meeting about white people and what would be done if they came to the Longhouse? The elder had called her white.

He was the elder she had held in highest esteem, the one who, only a few years ago, had given Gail her Indian name.

Gail had called her, sobbing into the phone, about the pain she felt when he centered her out in front of the other members gathered for the ceremonies. It also pained Gail, that not only had he questioned her and her blood quantum in front of the others, but he did it inside their Longhouse.

Emily thought of the fights between the church people and the ones who believed in the traditional ways. Now there were fights between those who believed in the traditional ways. Among these were some who were rejected because of the choices that parents and grandparents had made.

Emily shook her shoulders as if to get rid of the creepy feeling and thought. On with the story or it will never get written:

> "What if these so-called leaders and elders were "walking their talk." Would they be helping the men and women of the Nations learn about love? Perhaps the men and women would not be "growing out of love" or there wouldn't be so many marriage breakups. They wouldn't be abusing each other. Perhaps there wouldn't be homeless and battered people in the world. The elders, the preachers, and the leaders are missing something. What is it that they are missing? Perhaps it is the key to the puzzle. Could it be that they need to look inside? Could it be that they have gotten so grand in their own minds that they have forgotten the Creator? Perhaps when they learn to love themselves they can then each other. Perhaps until then they need to stay at home and bake bread." Continuing, Emily read the final paragraphs.
>
> "It is with heavy heart that I see the people of South America reacting like the people of this continent did

when the Europeans came to North America. I see that they too will soon be attacking each other for gold, for riches, and over their blood quantum. Acculturation isn't the question. It is the destruction of the spirit of the peoples so that they no longer carry the true meaning of the culture and traditions inside. "It is not the blood that is in your nation but the nation that is in your blood." (Sarah ElizaBeth Hill Wisdom of the Grandfathers 1992 Unpublished) Is this statement by Sarah ElizaBeth Hill something that we are paying attention to?

Internalized racism is running rampant in communities. The hatred that the indigenous people have for the Europeans is now spreading like a fungus in our own communities, and we are turning it on ourselves. There is little respect for anyone. How are the children to know who they are and not judge one another? Perhaps they are not to change. Perhaps they are to continue the way of their fathers, mothers, grandmothers, and grandfathers and eventually annihilate each other.

Emily thought of an incident at the band office just last week. She heard that the community social worker had ended up quitting in a huff. Apparently, she was working more than 60 hours a week for less than $35,000 a year. She had a B.A. in social work and was working on her Master's degree. She did not get the position she had originally applied for. A non-Native man got the job and was receiving a salary of $60,000 to do the work she was capable of doing.

She thought how ironic that was. Having someone else come in to take care of our families who does not know about our ways and then they pay him twice as much as a woman who lives in the community. Emily continued with her story.

"I, for one, don't want this to be part of the gifts I hand down to my great-grandchildren and their descendants. What do we do to provide a better world for the next seven generations? Perhaps we must stop the hurt and the anger between cultures. Could it be that we must stop judging and having one-up-manship? Is it possible that we could stop having the sexism, racism, classism, and ageism wars? All the wars? If we are to look at the other continents, we should use this continent as an example of what not to do. Yes, colonialism does have an effect on the other continents. It surely has damaged this one."

Emily sat back. She looked out at the Owl and saw an imagined nod of her beautiful white head. She knew that she had received an answer to her questioning–even if she didn't know what the questions were.

What will happen to the other couples of the world? Are South America and the other continents going to go the way of North America? Are the other women of the world going to end up like Carol–like me? Will they see that the world is spiraling down to destruction with the split marriages and the 'isms' that are in every house in the country? How will it end?

Perhaps they will read my story and think a little before they act. Could it be that they will learn from the mistakes of others? Maybe they will see that there is hope. Perhaps they will not read the story and continue as before. Then I will write a story about the destruction of man and how the world survived.

5

INTERNALIZED RACISM: THE SILENT OPPRESSION FROM WITHIN

"Internalized racism." I hadn't heard of the term until a few years before the publication of the first edition of Shaking the Rattle. Racism, according to the Oxford dictionary, is "belief in the superiority of a particular race; prejudice based on this. Antagonism towards people of other races."

Internalized racism carries the belief that the Caucasian race is superior to the Native race, or that certain Natives are superior to another group of their same race. There exists hostility between people of the same race. In other words, the belief that some or many Natives have is that the Native race is inferior to the whites or the dominant culture.

In our communities, as a result of the residential schools, colonialism, government plans, and the churches, we have a lot of internal racism. An example of this is the conflict between church adherents and the traditional people. There are the elected band council supporters against the traditional council supporters. Between the so-called full bloods and the mixed bloods. Between the full bloods and the Métis. Between the mixed bloods and the Métis. Reverse racism towards people of other races is also a symptom of internalized racism. People of colour, i.e. Blacks, Hispanics, and Asians are sometimes looked down upon by some Natives in the same way that the

Natives are looked down upon by some whites. Some Native people have adopted quite a few racist ways of the dominant culture. They now treat each other and other peoples of colour the way our people are treated – with contempt, indifference, and sometimes hatred.

Internalized racism stems from colonialism and oppression. It is part of the dominant culture's ways that we have adopted and carried for generations. Now our learned behaviour has resulted in pain, and we have turned against each other. It eats away at the spirit of the community and reaches outwards to the nations. Many of our own people are turning against people of the same nation because they do not come from the same community. For example, the Iroquois Confederacy, which is the Six Nations of Mohawk, Cayuga, Seneca, Oneida, Onondaga, and Tuscarora, have in recent times had bitterness between the nations and the communities within each nation.

I have been noticing bitterness arising in communities across North America between those who support the band councils and those who do not. The traditional councils claim that they have the true government and they are partly correct. They do if the land has not been sold out by the band councils. The sad part is that in some communities the band councils have control and the traditional councils are losing it to their own people. The fight is now between the people and not between the Indians and the whites.

This is a reflection of the illness in the individuals and the communities. The need for power and control is overshadowing the other needs in most communities. The spirit of the community becomes lost in the bitterness, the anger, the greed, and the hatred. Because of the internalized pain, the people can't hear each other. They gossip and fight rather than support each other, especially if they think differently.

The need for love and belonging has brought many of the people back to the communities. Another one of the government's ploys to divide and conquer was the establishment of Bill C31. The government established the "Indian Act" that took away the "Indianness" of a woman if she married a white man or a person without an Indian

ID number. They took away the "Indianness" of families that wanted to leave the reserves and territories to go to work if they did not want to live in the restricted areas. They developed the term enfranchisement. Many of the people in generations past have opted for the enfranchisement – some under coercion. The need for love and belonging is bringing people back to the reserves and territories, and they are being met with. "You don't belong here. What are you doing here? Who gave you the right?" Because of the decisions made by parents and grandparents, usually under duress, we have people suffering.

People in communities who have lived there all their lives are afraid. They fear that the blood will thin. "We will end up with white guys learning the language and traditions." The anger that is spewing out of the mouths in communities is directed at the children and grandchildren and great- or greater-grandchildren. Was it really their fault? Are they to blame for the government and the church's doings? I don't think so. It is not up to me to judge, but I do have an opinion. I think that if everyone took a look at their own family tree, became aware and proud of who they are, there would not be so much hatred and prejudice. Just like black hair, brown eyes, and "Indian complexion" the prejudice and hatred is passed down.

Some of our people changed. They became greedy like the European conquerors. Because of the past oppression, their lives became powerless and they tried to take control wherever possible, usually by dominating the women and children. That control, fear, greed, and hatred emanated out – not at the white church and the government – but at each other. It is like that today. I look for the lineage memory and wonder what was passed down from our ancestors? However, the will to survive is also passed down. The love of all creation is starting to come alive again. My hope is for the internalized pain to be healed in individuals so that communities may also heal before it is too late for the land to heal.

6

THE ESCAPE

Gail's heart was full of fear as she packed her belongings. Hands shaking, palms sweating, and legs wobbling like jelly; she walked, grabbing her children's clothes with a flurry. Her thoughts ran amuck and muddled through her brain as she tried to sort them. "He might return any minute now. Is he nearby, watching, waiting? If he comes back now, the terror from the night before will start all over." She straightened herself up. This could not continue. She would not live like that anymore. She would not live with fear controlling her every move. She would not let her children live like that anymore.

Dennis came home from the bar, the night before, drunk as usual. This time it was different. He didn't go to his room as he usually did. He had different plans. He came towards her. His darting eyes let her know he was not as drunk as she had suspected. His loud angry words lashed out at her, and his huge body loomed over her as he followed her from room to room, flicking his BIC lighter off and on. Off and on. Like a crazed man, he accused her of all the ugly, rotten, adulterous things that had been running through his deranged mind for weeks.

He grabbed her. His powerful hands around her throat squeezing tighter and tighter as she struggled for breath. Darkness enveloped her, her life seeping into the darkness. She heard a faint cry. It was not her voice. They were not her words. All she heard was a whisper.

"Don't daddy; please don't kill mommy. Please don't hurt her," the voice pleaded.

His daughter's words edged through his stupor into his consciousness. He released his grip on her throat. He staggered back, rocking back and forth on his heels, trying to make a decision.

Gail lay crumpled on the floor. Melodie, her daughter, bent over her. She placed her hands on her mommy's face and softly, gently rubbed her cheeks. "Mommy wake up, wake up, don't cry Mommy, Daddy won't hurt you anymore." With tears running down her cheeks, the little girl sat beside her mommy, her pajamas twisted and tangled as she kept calling to her mommy in her little frightened voice.

Slowly she stirred. The first thought that came to her and the only thing that mattered, was her little girl. Her groggy thoughts were of the safety of her daughter. She took her little girl to her bed, covered her and held her.

"Mommy, I'm so scared. Is Daddy going to light the house? What if he burns the house down with us in it?"

She tried to think of soothing words for her little girl, as she caressed her forehead. Nothing came but the little trickle of tears as she rocked her baby in her arms.

After the first whimper of the child died away, in the quietness of the room, she could hear his footsteps on the carpet as he came up the stairs... slowly... staggeringly... deliberately. The fear began again choking first in her stomach, then in her chest, and then at her throat. He came closer and closer to her room. Silence. And then, from the doorway, his voice like thunder demanded that she come to his room.

Her little girl stirred in her arms, clung to her and looked up at her with those deer-in-the-headlight eyes, asking her not to go. She tightly wrapped her arms around her daughter and snarled over her shoulder that she would come and see him when the child was asleep. He turned and left while mumbling to himself. She rocked the child in her arms, whispering soothing words to calm her, while the gyrating motion of fear curdled her stomach.

Later in the night, she crept into his room praying that he would be asleep. He was not. The sickening, sweet, honey poured from his lips as he forcibly took her into his bed. She felt nauseated. She held her breath. She turned her head from his rancid breath. Her stomach curdled with the fear that gripped her. She closed her eyes and let her mind steal away to the safety of another time and another place.

His rough and calloused hands grabbed her breasts, tore her blouse, and buttons flew as if in a hurry to be out of the way. He clutched, pinched, and prodded as if trying to make her flesh be part of him—his and his alone. Grappling with her belt, he dragged it from her jeans and tossed it at the wall. The zipper broke as he yanked and pulled to lower the fabric over her flesh. Poking and prodding with his fingers, leaving bruises and scratches over her body as he dragged her into the shower. Biting her lip, holding back screams, she succumbed to his manipulations, and her spirit evaporated into the steam. With her mind a blank, he mistook her submissions for willingness. Their stay in the shower could not rid her of the filth and the dirt she felt was embedded in her flesh. His satisfaction removed all of her life.

Once satisfied, he dragged her to his room. As she lay beside him, his words of their future together were his last as he passed into the deep sleep of a drunk. No movement could awaken him for another few hours. Stiffly she climbed from his bed and tiptoed up the stairs to her room. Quickly she dressed and lay again with her baby girl and tried to close her eyes. Sleep evaded her because of her terror that she would have to go through that again. She made her decision. She grabbed her sleeping child, left the room and the house and fled into the night. Like a river suddenly changing course, they left.

7

RELATIONSHIPS: THE TWO ROW WAMPUM

The Two-Row Wampum Belt is a contract or treaty signifying a deal or law or pact between the Iroquois and the Europeans. It was our written record of the treaty between two peoples, two governments, two distinct nations. It signified that each would have their own government, their own laws, and their own way of life. The Europeans would not interfere with ours and we would not interfere with theirs. It is said that the words were (paraphrased), "You stay in your canoe, and I'll stay in mine."

I see the Two-Row Wampum also used when describing a relationship, any relationship, not just between two governing bodies. The relationship between husband and wife, friend and neighbor, etc. It is not that I have my laws and you have yours, but we both have our own individual choices. We have our own truths, and we both follow the laws of the Creator.

The Two-Row Wampum applies when you look at the relationship of marriage whether it be through the church, the Longhouse or through your commitment to each other and the Creator. "I do not try to tell you what to do, and you do not tell me." We each have our own lives and we do what we can to uphold ourselves, to be true to our-selves and together we work at the marriage relationship. It is not a fantasy world out there either. You do have to work at a marriage. It is not always the romantic, fairy-tale life that you first experienced when you fell in love. When you make the commitment to be together, it is usually for life not just until something better comes along.

Knowing and loving and honouring the self first is being true to the self. Contrary to popular belief, that is not being selfish. If you do not know what you want out of life how can you tell your partner when she/he asks? If you don't know how to love and please your- self, how can you ask for what you want? If you do not know what makes you unhappy, then how can you decide if this person will be the one that you want in your life forever?

For example, I came to school in September. I met many nice people–one woman in particular with whom I struck up a friendship, and we started looking for an apartment together. We had decided that we were going to be roommates before we even talked. Finally, after a week or two of looking unsuccessfully I said, "Hey we don't even know if we can live together or not." So, we sat and talked. The long and short of it was we decided that we each wanted something different and got our own places within that very same week. If we had not talked, we each would have been miserable in a very short time or one would be giving up herself, her boundaries, her space, to compensate for the other.

Relationships are about boundaries. Relationships are about fighting and loving and working at keeping a friendship strong even if you have had a fight, argument, disagreement, or knock down drag 'em out war. Keeping the little person inside is safe, in spite of the connection to the person you are in the relationship with, is most important. "Above all else, to thine own self be true" applies here as it does in all relationships.

"Friends make better lovers" is an old saying that I heard a long time ago when I was a kid. I don't remember where I heard it, and I was little and didn't understand what that meant. Today I understand that to mean that if I can't be friends with the person I love and live with, then I won't be a good lover and neither will my partner. How can you make love to someone you don't like? A healthy, caring person cannot make love to someone they don't like. A person under the influence of alcohol and drugs may be able to have sex with someone just for the need to be held because they are lonely but if you are healthy, love, and care for yourself, then you would not be wanting to go to bed with someone you didn't like.

Remembering the Two-Row Wampum in all my relationships helps me and reminds me that everything doesn't always have to be my way. It's like the co-dependency thing that everyone talks about. I have to make sure that I am taking care of everything in my own life before I try to take care of yours, if I am to be a healthy, strong person. I cannot be true to myself or keep myself healthy and fit, if I'm spending all my time worrying about you, your friends, your family situations, your job, etc. ad infinitum.

Today, the focus is always outside. It has been that way for the past few generations because the Europeans and their puritanical "churchified" thinking brought their fear of everything, fear of nature to our communities. Fear of anything can cause us to look outside for the answers. Much of what happens in a family that is fear and shame related equates to not feeling safe. And much of what happens in what is called co-dependency is that we are not feeling safe in relationships – unsafe in either family, or friends, or even workplace. This can cause us to become compulsive, obsessive control freaks and often leads to addictions such as work addiction, compulsive eating and obsessive controllers. We focus outward and neglect ourselves to the point of shutting down our feelings which often results in abusive behaviour towards ourselves and others.

Traditionally the families in one clan lived together in one Longhouse. The grandmothers and grandfathers were valued people because they had all the teachings and the lessons. They were the doctors of philosophy, medicine, and theology. They continued to be valued human beings until they departed this land not because they were old, but because they earned the respect. They continued to follow those laws that the Creator set down, and they lived by the principles that resulted in the Two-Row.

The aunts and uncles disciplined the children in order to keep the relationships between parent and child in a harmonious balance. Everyone looked after each other's child. There was no distinction between yours and mine. All children were recognized as the children of the Creator, gifts to the people. Everyone took responsibility. No child was disrespectful enough to say "You can't tell me what to do; you aren't my mom/dad."

In the homes of the Europeans, the wives stayed home and looked after the children. Most families lived a rural lifestyle. These people came here and left their own parents back in the old country. Occasionally, if they could afford it, they hired a young woman. It was usually a family member, and she would work with the children while the women worked alongside the husband. They helped to build their children's homes when they got old enough to have their own families and share the farm. The parents then had their house, and the children had theirs on the same farm. Much of the family life was in isolation. The only examples that I hear of today that resembles extended families similar to ours are the Mennonites, Amish, and people of those religious sects.

Today the grandmothers and grandfathers in many cities and towns are placed in nursing homes. Mothers and fathers both work and children are in day-care. Or grandparents are staying home and raising their grandchildren because their children are out drinking and drugging. Or the adults are at bingo and/or the casinos while the little children are watching the babies. There is no unity, no home life and no stability. And we wonder why the kids are so troublesome and rebellious.

All forms of government, federal and provincial, have ignored and dishonored the Two-Row Wampum. Also, many personal relationships ignore it. Healing and recovery takes place on a personal level first. It is not going to work to go to a marriage counsellor if one person is still stuck in their pain.

Governments are not going to honour treaties and the Two-Row Wampum when they don't even recognize the people that first made the treaties. They still think of them as children – someone they have to look after and control – the thinking that came with their forefathers. And so too, it is not going to work to have the children in counselling if the parents are still acting out with dysfunction, being away, arguing, fighting, drinking, or drugging and all the other symptoms of unresolved trauma. Remember, children learn by watching their parents and other adults or those they perceive as adults.

It is our responsibility to make a better world for the next seven generations. According to Iroquois philosophy, all decisions made in the present should be made with the principal that it should benefit seven generations ahead. And we need to start with the self. Self-recognition, self-caring, self-healing, and with that comes the modeling for the children. The children can carry the steps forward to make a better world for their next seven generations. Just as in addictions, "You didn't become an alcoholic, (or compulsive eater, or work addict or sex addict, or gambler) overnight so don't expect that you are going to get better overnight." We are not going to make the governments listen overnight. We are not going to make strong healthy marriages overnight, and we are not going to stop juvenile rebellion overnight.

8

THE QUESTIONS

S uddenly I walk towards the phone, and then I go back and sit. I rub my hands over my eyes and up through my hair. My back braces against the couch, and my heels press into the tile floor. I can't see and I can't stop shaking. Getting up, I pace the floor. What do I do?

I never understood how any man, myself included, could brutally abuse a woman and why would a woman put up with it? Yet here I am just like all the rest. Shit, I am a pig, an animal, a slut, a whore. I pace wishing again that I could take back the pain. What did Gramma used to say? Wish in one hand and shit in the other. Wonder what the hell that meant? How could my mind jump like that? Carol, where did you go? How could I hurt you like that? Everything was going so great. Then, oh shit, if only you were here to listen; if only you hadn't left. I don't want to be here, alone, to go through this. I don't want to remember last night.

I was gentle at first. I caressed your body with a gentle feather-like touch. I remember the soft kisses that we gave each other and the gentle prodding.

Shit, now all I can remember is the pounding, thrusting animal that I became. What happened to me? Where did that rage come from? What was I thinking? I'll never forget the pained look when the light left her eyes, and she was like a beaten puppy. I don't blame her for leaving. I wish to God I could leave. Nothing will ever take away my feeling of disgust. I knew I couldn't look at her again without feeling myself shrivel inside.

I wonder why Carol insisted that I call Aunt Jenny? Surely to God she doesn't think I'll tell Aunt Jenny what I did. She must have thought something though or she wouldn't have insisted. Now what do I do? I already told Jenny I'd come by for a visit, but I'd rather just crawl away and die. I'd be better off if I could just disappear. That was some conversation at five o'clock this morning. I was stupid to call at that hour. I couldn't even tell her what happened. All I could say was, "Aunt Jenny I need help." I had wimped out.

The deed is done. She's expecting me. I need to do something. I wouldn't have gotten myself into this shit if I were okay. Maybe I need more therapy.

I better get my ass in gear if I'm going to make it to Jennie's house by five. I got just enough time for a shower and maybe some coffee. Jeez, I haven't even slept; hope I can drive that far without falling asleep. Maybe I better have a double espresso instead. Where's my razor? Ow, damned these water taps. If it ain't freezing, it's scalding.

The hot water feels good. My body aches as much as my insides. If only this water would wash away the pounding, thrusting, jabbing I see constantly and wash away the pain in my heart.

How long have I known Aunt Jennie? It seems she's been around since I can remember. We were neighbours. I remember running to her house and staying there a couple of times when my parents fought.

That shower felt good. Can a rough towel rub the skin off a person? Peel the top layer off like a grapefruit, and see what's underneath. I wonder why Aunt Jennie became a stockbroker on Wall Street? She always seemed like the person in the neighborhood who would have been a great mom. Some kid would have been lucky. I was lucky she was there for me.

Damn this traffic. Why do I always pick Friday night to go to New York and try to drive in this crazy city? The drive, as slow as it is, will give me the opportunity to see the old neighborhood again. I wonder if the old pizza parlor is still there. I live only an hour out- side the city, and I don't get into town more than once a year.

Mom tried so hard to raise us right. She did everything to make us responsible for ourselves. I hated her at the time for that. I wanted my mom to do everything for me the way Gramma did for Uncle Josh. She was even washing his clothes when he was twenty-eight. Mom made me wash my clothes when I was twelve. Mom was really great, if only she were here now so I could tell her.

This old neighborhood hasn't changed much. There's the brown-stones, the deli and the florist shop. Hey, the pizza joint is still there. I wonder how often I picked up flowers for Mom, after Dad would slap her around, and get myself some pizza on the way back? That old bastard would never think of bringing her flowers. There's Aunt Jennie's place. It's been three years since I saw her. Wonder if things have changed much? Carol was always after me to call and go see her. The last time we saw each other was at Nancy's and John's wedding on Shelter Island. Guess I need to apologize right off for being gone so long.

I had just always thought of her as Aunt Jennie. The beautiful woman with the model-like figure and long blonde hair. I had often wondered how she could be my aunt when she was blonde and Mom and Dad were both so dark. Mom had explained she had been her best friend since school, and they just became close like sisters. I even remember telling Mom when I was eight that I should marry Aunt Jennie so she could always be part of our family.

Four forty-five, I'm a bit early. The place still looks the same. These flowers are beautiful. The lady upstairs must still do the gardening. Am I at the right place? Yeah, 27 Burlington Crescent. There's Aunt Jennie in the doorway. She still looks the same, and she still has her girlish figure.

"Aunt Jennie you look great."

"Hello Dan, welcome. It's been a long time."

"This place hasn't changed." *I never would have thought of making a library out of the foyer though. Great idea. Books, pictures, and plants fill every space, nook and cranny. I wonder how long ago she did this remodeling?*

"It feels so warm and cozy here, Aunt Jennie."

"Thanks, Dan, and you look great. Come on, let's go and have some tea."

The kitchen looks warmer and sunnier than I remember. More modern–it even has a bigger window and lighter paint. Wow, even a glass-topped table and wrought-iron furniture. Ah, but the old wicker sofa with the big, soft, downy cushions is still here. Aunt Jennie's tastes have changed.

"Aunt Jennie, I see you're using the good china and silver tea service. Just like when I was a kid. Remember how I always pretended that you were the queen, and you invited me over for tea?"

"Yes, and how I would have to tell you stories of the knights of the round table while you had your tea."

"I wonder whatever happened to that little boy, Aunt Jennie?" The words slipped from my lips before I could stop them. She seemed not to notice. She just patted my arm and led me to the chair.

"Sit with me a while, and let the traffic jitters calm down. It must have been busy today. The Governor was in the city touring so they have extra security out."

Her hair, it's darker and streaked with grey and silver. It looks nice with the streaks of blonde. "Your hair, a new style?"

"Yes, I decided that I needed a new look. I was tired of the long blonde curls so I cut it. Do you like it?"

"Very much." The kitchen has a new look to it. It must be the new table and chairs or - no maybe it's the new, coppery cooking utensils hanging from the black wrought-iron wheel above the island counter top. Hell, I'm only stalling. It's been three years since I saw her and over five since I've been here to her house. Of course it's changed and so has she.

"So, Don, tell me, how's the job? Do you still have your dancing shoes polished?"

"Yes, Aunt Jennie. The show is great. We travelled all over the U.S. and even hit Vancouver and Toronto before we did a tour of Europe."

Aunt Jennie always knew how to make me feel comfortable here. I feel like a little kid again. I feel like I just ran over here from home after seeing the beginning of another battle. It's so safe with her.

"Remember when I used to always run over here? Did you ever get sick of me? Didn't you just wish I would go away and find someone else to cry to? Seemed like every weekend I had to come over here 'cause they'd be fighting."

"I never thought of you as a nuisance. I always wanted you and your mom to be safe. That's why my door was open to you kids and her and is still open for you now."

She always made it so easy for me to talk to her. She was always a good listener. How can I tell her I raped my girl friend? It would devastate her. It's not something you just blurt out. Like "I missed you Aunt Jennie" and "oh, by the way, I raped Carol last night." No, I have to find some other way. Shit, I don't even want to talk about it.

"Aunt Jennie, remember the time my Mom kicked Dad out, and he wouldn't go so we did?"

"I remember lots of times when your mom would take you kids and leave because of your dad's drinking. She tried often not to be around when he came home from work on Fridays so they wouldn't fight."

"They always fought. Do you know that I ran away about six times before I was ten years old?"

"Now that, I didn't know."

"Yep! Once I got picked up by the cops. They brought me home, and I promised never to do it again if they wouldn't wake up Mom and Dad and tell them. They never did, I guess. I asked Mom before she died. She said she never knew. I didn't want her to know because she had so many other things to worry about."

Jennie's fine bone china cups and saucers suit her. She is elegant and her things are so much like her. I see she has a print of Monet! Wonder what she did with the paintings I gave her as a child? I couldn't leave them at home. Dad probably would have burnt them. He was always taking Mom's books and burning them saying we needed fuel for fire. Could have burned the damned ole money he spent on booze for all the good it did.

I rose from my chair to go and look out the window. It overlooks the yard next door with all the herbs and vegetables one needs for a good salad. Too bad it's the neighbour's. I see she still collects pottery. *Wonder what all these pieces are and where they came from?*

"Aunt Jennie, what's this?" I ask, picking up this brown and white piece trying to kill time.

"It's a wedding vase."

Stalling and making small talk isn't working. I need to get the conversation where I feel comfortable. Ask her questions. Start small talk again. Anything so my mind will not go back to Carol.

"Aunt Jennie, are there any good memories you have of when we lived next door?"

"I have lots of good memories. Especially the dance recitals and plays you did and Lily's debates. Your mom and I went to all the school functions. I hated seeing your family in trouble all the time, but I couldn't do anything about it. I just had to be there for you. I figured one day she would leave. Sure enough she did."

"Yeah, but the damage was already done by then."

"What do you mean?"

I've done it now. I've said more than I intended. I don't want to spill the beans like this. I want to visit first. Shit. I sit and just as quickly stand up and start pacing. Where are the words when you need them?

"Aunt Jennie, is there any sign of insanity in my family that you know of?"

"Not that I know of. What's going on with you? You don't just come over here after a few years and ask me if there's insanity in your family. What's wrong?" *I can't just tell her I raped Carol. Have to think of something else.* I stopped pacing and stood by the counter, accidentally bumping my head on a frying pan hanging low over the counter.

Sitting again I look over the kitchen decor and start to straighten the place mat and the tea service. Anything to occupy my mind. She reaches over and grabs my hands.

"What's wrong?"

"Well I've been going to a therapist back home, and to a twelve-step group a few years back. The therapist suggested a group called Adult Children of Alcoholics and then Al-Anon. They are both for people who have had alcoholics in their lives. Everything was going really well for a few years." I stand up again and the wrought-iron chair falls backwards with a clang on the Spanish tile floor. The sound jars my memory.

Suddenly I am back in my living room at the age of twelve. A frying pan flies across the room. Mom is sitting at the table crying. Dad yells with his arm raised again. I can't take it anymore.

"Stop," I scream. "Just stop it."

Both look at me. My baby sister crawls out from under the kitchen table and clings to my leg.

"You quit hitting Mom," I yell. "You got no right to hit any of us. You're nothing but a... a... I saw you in bed with another woman when Mom went to visit Gramma. You got no right treating us that way when you do things like that. You should just leave."

Placing the chair upright and standing next to me Aunt Jennie asks again, "What's wrong?"

"I got to thinking as I was driving here. I remember how much I hated my dad when I was a kid because I would see my mom with bruises or because I would hear them arguing. I never want to be like him. I just remembered all the abuse and wondered if maybe he was just completely crazy."

"Dan, I remember the pain you and your family went through. But as far as I know, he wasn't crazy. The alcoholism made him do things he wouldn't have done if he were sober."

"Did you know that I saw my dad in bed with another woman when Mom wasn't home?"

"Yes."

"I was only about twelve when that happened. Mom and Dad were fighting, and I couldn't take it anymore. I just screamed for them to stop and then blurted out that I saw Dad in bed with another woman. I still don't know if Mom believed me. I heard Dad pleading with her to listen. He was asking her if she believed me or him. She wouldn't answer. And then I felt bad because I didn't want to hurt her."

"I know she believed you. She couldn't do anything at the time, but she believed you."

"I kept asking her to leave every time she got beat up, or he came home drunk, or when he never came home, but she never would."

"Yes, I know it was trying for you all. She just didn't have it in her to leave then."

"I know now, but I never could understand why she stayed with him. He hurt her so much. He hurt all of us."

I walk around the kitchen. The tile is shiny and new, a coppery burnt orange colour, and the wallpaper picked up the flecks of dark green in the tiles. Seeing the wallpaper reminded me of the curtains in Carol's bedroom. Damn. I pounded the wall and then turned to Aunt Jennie.

"Aunt Jennie, the counsellor has been asking many questions about the abuses in our home. I remember some of it yet something is missing."

"Like what? I know that you came over here every opportunity just to play, and other times when you felt you were in danger."

"Oh, I don't know. There is anger coming up in me and sometimes I can't control it. He was asking if there was other abuse other than the physical abuse that we went through."

"Well, your mom never talked about her intimate details – you know the husband and wife intimacy – but there may have been other abuses. I know that I have heard that in alcoholic marriages sometimes there is what they call marriage rape."

Oh great. There may be a history of rape. Just what I need to know. But I am not an alcoholic. I don't even drink or use drugs. I can't afford it. What the hell, how does that affect me?

"I don't remember any of that, 'course I wouldn't know if he raped her or not would I?"

"No. You wouldn't. If your father was drunk and she didn't want to start a fight–afraid of waking you up–she might have given in without desire and consent."

"Could he have raped her in any other way?"

"Well I'm not sure. Not being a therapist or anything, but rape inside a marriage isn't necessarily violent. It could mean that she didn't want to be intimate when he was drinking and him not listening, or he had been verbally abusive. Sometimes men only think of their needs and don't listen when the woman says no."

"I guess we'll never know."

"No – we can't ask them. He was an angry man. He became an orphan at two, and he was raised by all sorts of relatives who were mostly alcoholic as well. People in the helping profession would say that he probably didn't have a chance. You know that many problems come from being raised in alcoholic families."

"Yeah, that's what I been told – in my group counselling. That's why I'm asking all these questions."

Jennie stands next to me as I stare out the large picture window that overlooks the herb garden next door. She puts her arm around my waist. We used to be the same size; now it seems like she has shrunk. We stand together quietly as the clock chimes six in the hall. Tears drip down my cheeks.

"I miss Mom so much."

"Yes dear, I know. I miss her too. Have you talked with your sister lately?"

"No, she's been in Australia since she graduated from university. She's studying Aboriginal Law, and it will take her another two years. She wrote at Christmas. Asked me to come visit."

"Are you going to go?"

"Someday, Aunt Jennie. Someday."

"It's so great to have you here, Dan. It's been too long." "Yeah, it's great to see you too."

She just stands there with her arm around my waist. She has a great way of not noticing my tears. As a child, she would let me cry and would go puttering about. Now, she gives me the same courtesy. I guess she doesn't want to embarrass me. I never saw Dad cry – even when his aunt died. When I had asked Dad why he didn't cry he had said, "Tears are for sissies." She gives me a hug and says,

"I'm going to fix us a light supper. I need to eat and I would love your company. How about some fruit or a salad?"

I just nod my head and continue to stare out the window. Turning around a bit later I take in the view of the collection of spoons on the wall rack.

"Aunt Jennie, do you think that Dad loved us?"

"I think that he loved you and your family very much. He just had a disease and much pain inside. He couldn't show it in a good way."

"Come, sit and have some supper with me. I hate eating alone, and it's surprising how often I do it."

I sit. The fruit salad is in front of me, and I try to eat. The pieces of food have a hard time going past the lump in my throat. Toast points are easier to swallow after I dunk them in the tea, the way she taught me as a boy.

Mom taught me to cry. She convinced me to go to counselling, and she even helped me a lot with this pain. Why did this happen? Why, after all my love for Carol, her love for me, why did I do that rotten, despicable thing. . . Shit, I'm no better than him. I'm a fuckin' monster just like him.

"I have so many questions. Sometimes I feel like a monster. I don't want to hate my dad. I really loved him. I get so confused at times. I feel like a traitor even going to therapy and to the group counselling."

"Dan, you're not a monster and neither was your father. He was an alcoholic. He was sick. Remember the times he was sober? Remember the times you had fun with him?"

"Yeah, but I must have been about three. I don't remember him being proud of me. I don't remember him being at my dance recitals. He didn't want me doing anything but work and play football. I didn't want to play football. Just because he was a football star in college he thought I should be. I couldn't. I wanted to be a dancer. I always wanted to be a dancer. All I remember was the pain of him calling me fag. I didn't even understand the word, but I knew it wasn't good by the way he looked when he said it. Now I know."

I get up, pick up my dishes from the table and take them to the sink. She reminds me that she had a dishwasher when I start to run the water to wash the dishes. I dry my hands and go back to the table.

"Do you think that we can inherit all that garbage?"

"Well, Dan, it seems to me that you and Lily have done quite well for yourselves to become what you always wanted to be. You both have careers, and I don't see any alcoholism in your lives. You can, you know, have the compulsions to hide your feelings. The desire to find some way of hiding your feelings. I'm sure that your therapist has given you all kinds of information."

"Yeah we talked about the effects of growing up in alcoholic homes. How we can even become control freaks or become someone who is afraid to let other people do things."

"What else?"

"Well you can inherit qualities like that, or you can use other substances instead of dealing with problems. You know like food, gambling, work. I guess I was just wondering if I could become angry like him – you know his rage, his abusing us and in particular Mom."

"Your father didn't have any help. He chose to drink whenever he had pain. Then it became an addiction–his body couldn't live without it–and he eventually died of it. Sometimes counselling helps, and sometimes it doesn't. Each person has to make their own path."

"How come you never went into counselling and helped people. "You're so good at it?" I didn't learn all this stuff in school. I learned it from going to therapy for myself. I also grew up in an alcoholic home. I had a mother who was alcoholic, and my father just up and left us one day. My drive to make things better gave me the drive to get my education and the good job I have. This compulsion to control things drove me to control so much in my life that I ended up alone. My therapist helped me to understand that it comes from the childhood issues of trying to make things better so Mom wouldn't drink and so Dad wouldn't leave. I controlled things so much that the man I loved left."

"So I won't become abusive like him? Being in therapy and all."

"There is a good chance that you will eventually end up in a healthy marriage and have two-point-five children. I'm kidding, Don. There is a very good chance that you will be happy even though you were a victim."

What a label. Victim. "I'm a survivor, Aunt Jennie."

"That you are."

"All that shit I saw happening at home; it's hard going through the therapy. It's hard remembering it."

"You'll do fine, Dan. You get help for what you remember and then the other memories come up. You remember more and get more help. Then after you integrate the learning into your life you remember more."

"It's too bad we can't have a magic wand to remove all of it at once," I say smiling at her.

"You cannot heal everything at once. You can only heal what you're ready to remember. And the Creator is the one to decide what you can handle with his help."

"You know, Aunt Jennie, when I was in the shower this morning, I was thinking about all the stuff I learned as a boy growing up. I saw my mom and dad and all that shit. I heard all that crap about how men act, and yet, I never felt that I wanted to be like that. So I did everything I could to not be like my dad."

"We can only learn as children from watching. We see how our parents act, and we learn our roles that way. When we get older, we hear other things and we learn other things. It is in our nature to be loving and compassionate human beings. We see other ways and live with abuse and we get confused. We end up holding in feelings until they build into a rage that explodes and we have no control over when, how, and where it explodes. That's what happened to your dad and many other men."

"That's for dammed sure."

"All you have been through is something you can heal. Remember you have already been through the painful times. The memories won't kill you. You are adaptable. Otherwise you would not have survived till today. Work through the fear. The Creator won't give you anything more than you TWO can handle together for the day."

"I get so scared that I will end up like all the other men that I have known. I don't want to be a wife beater or hold my feelings in. And I sure as hell don't want to walk around thinking that women are only good for two things. Cooking and sex."

"I know that under all that pain your dad was a good, loving man. And your mom was not a saint. She had her faults too, but she taught you how to love yourself. She supported you in your choices. If you continue to remember her love and support and work towards forgiveness you will be okay. Forgiveness is a process, not a goal."

We finish our visit and I give Aunt Jennie a hug. I really did miss her. I promise that I will come back soon. I mean it and as I get in my car I also promise to send her tickets for the next show I will be dancing in.

As I drive back to the apartment, I recall our conversation and think of the work that I have done. I miss Mom, and Lily, and occasionally, I even miss Dad. I remembered the time when we went to the ball game and Dad fell on the bleachers and got up yelling, "You're out." I was so embarrassed. Yet now I smile and think how neat it would be to have him here to go to a ball game with.

9

SEXUAL ABUSE

Europeans came to the Americas with their beliefs that not only were women and children to be owned but that the church and the education system were best for the "savages." They removed the Indigenous children from their Native communities and homes and placed them in the residential schools. These children were then "parented" by nuns, priests, and often single, female teachers who were inexperienced in child rearing.

The puritanical thinking and the strong influence of the church dictated that sex was a taboo subject. All of this brought shame to the once free, healthy Natives about their dress, their bodies, and their parenting skills. They felt shame for their acceptance of sex as a natural part of life. Subsequently, the children learned shame.

Before European contact, the Indigenous people of North America had belief systems that were a reflection of their understanding and perception of their world. To them, the moon was "our grandmother," the sun was "our elder brother," and the earth was "our mother." The relationship to all things in creation was one of kinship.

With European contact came a new set of beliefs and world view. These beliefs conflicted with the Indigenous beliefs. Populations grew and a majority culture with its own set of beliefs emerged. Natives struggled to retain both a cultural identity and a system of beliefs unique to themselves. The once open, honest teachings were forced underground along with their medicines, songs, and ceremonies.

Parents lost hope when their children left for residential school. They turned to the bottle to dull the pain of loneliness and sense of failure. Children returned for holidays and summer breaks and found their parents either intoxicated or gone. They had nowhere to turn. They internalized their pain and shame along with the abandonment and the sense that "it was their fault that their parents were no longer there." Anger began to emerge as the dominant feeling, with apathy a close second.

Parents were unavailable. Nuns and priests weren't good role models as parents (because of the vow of celibacy, they did not have children.) The main function of the Catholic church was to convert and control. Sexual abuse became the norm. Catholic teachings stress celibacy for the nuns and priests to the outside world, yet few practice it. The children in the residential school were subjected to sexual and physical abuse. When a person of the church abuses, or abuse takes place in a church setting, this results in spiritual abuse. Now there is physical, spiritual, and sexual abuse. Couple that with the shame and the secrecy and confusion results. We now have emotional and mental abuse on top of the sexual, physical, and spiritual abuse.

These children, removed from families, communities, and nations are emotionally abused as well. Their parents were no longer available. They were forbidden to speak their language, and some totally blocked the language to adopt English or French as a survival mechanism. When they returned to their communities, the one or two people they could get their support from – their grandparents – could not understand the new language. They now had a communication problem. These children were isolated in their own communities.

Children having experienced abuse were no longer children. Teachings about sexuality was a taboo subject within the church and the residential school. Self-esteem was low or non-existent. These young people turned to alcohol and/or sexual acting out as coping mechanisms. Early pregnancy occurred. They were children with babies. They didn't know how to be parents. You learn parenting by watching your parents. These children never had parenting. Their upbringing was regimented boarding school conditioning. As a result, we have generations of children experiencing abuse. We also have the puritanical teachings around sex. For example, sex is a man's thing; men enjoy it; it's a woman's duty; it's dirty; save yourself for your husband. Also there usually was no mention of sex and sexuality. There was no nurturing and teaching of women's roles and men's roles as there once was.

Along with the lack of teachings around sexuality and sexual roles was the taboo around homosexuality. Homosexuals were once a natural part of the communities. They each had special roles. They were not ostracized or degraded. With the landed immigrants came their fears or puritanical teachings that were against homosexuals. Now there is the strong homophobic themes running through the communities. Contrary to popular belief, you do not become homosexual through osmosis. You either are or you're not. It is not contagious.

In her book *Awakening Your Sexuality - A Guide for Recovering Women*, Stephanie Covington quotes Barbara G. Walker of The Women's Encyclopedia of Myths and Secrets: (San Francisco, Harper & Row 1983: 535-536):

> *"Female homosexuality was generally regarded as a virtually unthinkable threat in patriarchal societies. Christian Europeans regarded lesbianism as a crime without a name, and sometimes burned lesbians alive without a trial."*

With this legacy, the need to deny and to conform to the dominant heterosexual model ran deep and communicated loudly. Sexual teachings were once a natural part of life just as healthy parenting once was in our communities. Shame was not a part of sexuality or sexual roles. That came with the European teachings and the abuses. Lack of sexual teachings was and still is a devastating form of abuse. At one time, Iroquois communities were matrilineal. The human relationship in relation to Mother Earth was in all respects the same as the relationship one had to their own mother. The mother cared for and provided substance for life as does the earth.

Because of the abuses suffered in residential schools and/or the lack of nurturing from the natural mother (when, out of despair she turned to drink), both men and women started to lose respect for the mother or the females in the community. In addition, at this time, the European and their form of government forced the people to follow the *Indian Act* and change from the matrilineal society to the patrilineal. Men lost respect for women. Women lost respect for themselves. Children became confused.

There was not only lack of teachings, nurturing, and respect, there was now the battle between the sexes. On one hand they were hearing that Iroquois were a matrilineal society and how important the roles of women were. On the other hand, they were seeing abuse, feeling abuse, and acting out the abuse against women and each other.

Today in all communities there is sexual abuse, spousal abuse, and child abuse. There are homes for battered women, there are homes for battered spouses, and there are countless homes for abused children. There are homes for children deemed unmanageable by parents or for children whose parents are unable to care for them "properly." Are these much different from foster homes or orphanages? All these homes are the result of the oppression, the church domination, and the patrilineal government.

Sexual recovery is difficult in today's society. Sex is emphasized or promoted with commercials and ads. Sex is mistaken for intimacy, and it is used for power. It is a bargaining tool between spouses, and a commodity. Sex is still a secret in many homes, and sex is considered shameful. There is only support for those who have recognized their sexual abuse or those who admit to being addicts.

Sexuality is human participation in creation and creativity. Procreation is the need for our species to continue. Sexuality and spirituality are interwoven. Our spirituality is our core. Sexuality is our identity. We are spiritual beings who identify as sexual human beings.

According to Kellogg and Harrison, in their book *Finding Balance,* other people do not make us sexual, but they can damage our sexuality. They have a list of over thirty sexual abuse and/or sexual boundary violations such as a lack of information about sex, puberty, and our bodies. Also, exposure to pornography, excessive joking, sexual innuendos, sexualized rage, jealousy, and fighting are just a few.

> *"Abuse creates a shame response that is difficult to label, expose, express, embrace and deal with, so it becomes internalized. All internalized shame becomes sexual shame because it affects how we feel about our bodies and about being men and women." (Kellogg & Harrison 1991:127)*

All abuse is sexual abuse because it affects us as men and women in a negative way. It damages our responses to ourselves. We can no longer trust and be spontaneous. We end up repeating the abuse with inappropriate sexual behaviour and oft times entering into the same kind of relationships that we left because we were feeling abused. Or we end up abusing those smaller than ourselves.

The clan system in our nations was not only a political mechanism; there was also a family system. It was a way of preventing incest. All members of one clan are related, no matter what nation you came from. This protected you from intermarrying with relatives. A bear clan member is related to all bear clan members. Today, incest is the most common form of child sexual abuse nationwide in all cultures.

> *"Sexual abuse – incest is any sexual contact between a child and a person who is closely related or who is perceived to be*

related, including step-parents, and live-in partners of parents." (Kellogg & Harrison 1991)

It also includes anyone who is an authority figure such as a teacher, a therapist, a minister, an employer, a doctor, or a close friend of the family, etc. This includes anyone the child trusts for life-giving nurturing and caretaking.

Mainstream society has pretended to have a taboo on incest and other forms of abuse. There has never been a taboo on incest. In many cultures, arranged marriages most often see marriages between relatives. The taboo has been on talking about incest and on prosecuting the offending adult.

Rape and incest are more common in our cultures that we care to admit. Only about one in nine hundred rapists go to court, and the average sentence is about six months. The court system is repeatedly traumatizing the rape victim. This disrespect is like being raped again.

The most common form of rape is friend, date, or acquaintance rape. Marital rape is most often not acknowledged or recognized and nearly always ignored. Marital rape is most often overlooked because of the idea that "it's the wife's duty and the man has his needs."

> *"Whenever a person says no at any point in time, and the no is not respected or listened to, it is sexual molestation: rape. This includes situations when a person is unable to say no due to confusion, naiveté, ignorance, vulnerability, impairment, special learning problems, being sick, drunk, passed out or in a one-down position." (Kellogg & Harrison 1991: 128)*

The original teachings in most, if not all societies, were that mothers, aunties, and grandmothers raised the children until the age of puberty. They taught with love and nurturing. Children learned by watching the interchange between the sexes. Children learned about love, caring, and feelings, especially how to cry and release feelings. At puberty, boys went off and learned from the men – the fathers, uncles, and grandfathers. In this way the men learned about parenting and their feminine side. There are two sides to each of us. We as women have the male side inside of us as well as the female side. The same with men. The male side is the doing side, the action side. The female side is the feelings side, the emotions. Living with men and women in community allowed children to learn all aspects of themselves, to grow with healthy self-esteem. Feelings were not shamed, and I doubt that boys stopped hugging or accepting hugs when they reached the age of five, or seven, or even twelve. Men were demonstrative with their feelings and were loving, caring and sharing human beings.

During the time that boys spent with the women, they were not without the love and the attention of the men in their lives. Because they were in clan systems everyone lived in community. There was a strong, loving interchange and the children saw this. Remember I said earlier that you learn to be a parent from watching your parents. You also learn respect and honour from watching your parents– how they treat each other as husband and wife. Males learn about their sexuality from their interchange with the women in their lives. Females learn this from their interchange with the men in their lives – their father and uncles. If the man feels good about himself as a male and respects women, his daughters will grow to be healthy, strong women. They will be sure of themselves, with great self-respect and will choose a partner that they will respect, and vice versa. The males will have the same opportunity with their moms, aunties, and grandmothers.

Because of the confusion in child rearing with Christian influence, men have been steered away from feelings. Or I should say they learned not to show feelings–any feelings but anger. In the book *Finding Balance*, Kellogg and Harrison state: "Men are not born rapists. They are learned rapists. Men are taught to compete and win in all aspects of their life including sex and love."

Man has distorted Christ's teachings and written and rewritten the Bible many times. With new ideas for control, and another idea for gaining riches, the Bible has been changed. With these changes came more fear and anger. With these changes came wars and more wars. Men were sent off to fight and kill. Part of war games was also rape and dishonesty.

Men have not been taught intimacy; they have been taught that sex is love, sex is intimacy, and sex is power. Society and the media teach with movies and advertisement that women are to be treated with disrespect, degradation, and forceful, rough treatment. Sexual abuse offenders are usually victims themselves. They have identified with their abuser from childhood and modeled themselves after that abuser. They then abuse and use their power to control others. They thrive on the power and the fear that they instill.

We do very little to change things because most of us have experienced some sort of sexual molestation. Rape always involves a power differential – incest is the form of rape that involves a power differential and authority. When women live in fear of further abuse or threatened abuse, they change their schedules; they look for ways to live in a protected cocoon, becoming men haters, or they end up repeating the pattern in their lives by marrying into abuse. They continue to live in abusive situations and raise their children in those situations. Children learn what they see and the cycle is perpetuated.

We confuse sex with love and completely ignore intimacy. Intimacy comes with healing or sexual recovery. It comes with healing sexual, emotional, and spiritual trauma. Our healing in those aspects brings us closer to be who we were meant to be and closer to the Creator. Our love for self and the Creator can then flow out to others. Many of us who have experienced sexual abuse are still able to find intimacy and can still function sexually. Sometimes we just can't find sexuality and intimacy in the same relationship.

Sexual abuse gives us a false maturity. We lose our childlike self. We act like sexually sophisticated adults but feel like small, inadequate, immature, vulnerable children at times. We aim to be invisible. If we aren't noticed, we won't be abused. We feel dirty, damaged, and responsible. Often we take more than one bath or shower a day trying to wash away the dirty feeling that just won't go away. Some people dissociate, repress, triangulate, have memory loss, and fear the anger inside. "If I allow my anger to come out I'll explode; or if I allow myself to get angry, I can't be responsible for what will happen." Fear and shame control our lives.

For many of us, we don't recognize fear as an emotion because we have always had it, always lived with it. It is part of us. Sometimes people create a crisis in the present out of fear, because looking at the past that has been denied for so long is terrifying. We will do anything to keep from being in any situation that will remind us of the abuse.

> "According to an expanded definition of sexual abuse, a child who is given no privacy in the bathroom or is repeatedly tickled until he or she cries is being sexually abused. A girl who is subjected to family members' comments about her breasts or a young boy who endures jokes about the size of his penis is being sexually abused. A spouse exposed to pornography or forced into sexual activity by his or her partner without consent is being sexually abused. And a child used for the sexual pleasure of any adult is being sexually abused." (Grof 1993:50)

Where there is alcoholism or drug abuse there is often sexual abuse. From the research done by therapists working with women and men with eating disorders there have also been signs of sexual abuse. It is prevalent everywhere, especially when you look at the media and the ad campaigns. Anywhere that a person's body is used for exploitation, there is sexual abuse.

The papers cry out with people's rage over sex murders, attacks by men, and all the abuse in today's society. The way to stop the violation is for the men and women to take responsibility for themselves, their health in all areas, and to start raising healthy children. Healing the trauma from the oppression of other cultures and from the internalized oppression can lead to healthy parents raising healthy children. It will not happen in the next few years, but why wait to start? The sooner we start; the sooner we will see results. Soon we will not have to have candlelight vigils for victims like Melanie Carpenter, who was kidnapped and murdered; and the women at the college in Montreal who were gunned down. Soon we will have safety. It starts with you – your recovery, your health, your children.

10

THE PERILOUS JOURNEY

"**S**ix weeks off work or I hospitalize you," were the words she heard from her doctor. Shocked but relieved for she had imagined all sorts of ailments. As Gail drove away from the place that had been her home for over a year and a half, she remembered all the pain that she encountered.

The snow fell gently as the sun set over the lake. To the left, gold lights danced on the steel-grey water as she sped along the highway. She felt gratitude inside her chest for the beauty that fell before her as she drove. Gratitude swelled inside and felt as enormous as the mountains that towered to her right. She drove, remembering the day at the doctor's office.

Gail had walked slowly out of the office. Dr. Neibing, a gentle man, had spoken in a calming voice.

"What you are suffering from is Post Traumatic Stress Disorder, and you can drive yourself to death if you don't change. Sleep when you want, eat when you want, and take walks in the fresh air. You will not lie awake at night, if you take naps during the day," he said. "Contrary to popular belief, sleep begets sleep." Those had been the kindest words she could ever have heard from him. She had been grateful for the drug-free therapy and freedom from hospitalization.

She now focused on the road. Gail gasped for breath at every turn. Her excitement at the beauty of the snow-laden trees and ice-capped rocks soon turned to anxiety as the darkness settled in and it began to snow harder. The news of the diagnosis had surprised yet relieved her. Driving in the heavy snow, she recalled the words, Post Traumatic Stress Disorder . . . had she been in a war? Maybe. The last few months had been rough. Gail remembered how weak she had been when she had left the doctor's office, barely making it, walking the short distance to her car. She had had to go home and lie down. Her doctor had been so kind to her and had given some relief and hope.

Gail clutched the wheel concentrating on her driving, yet the memories were relentless. She recalled how she had gotten the job. She had quit her job at the counselling centre, and that same night she had received a phone call. It had been from the Executive Director of the new treatment centre asking her to send her resume. Gail had gotten the job. She had thought, for sure, a person from their own area would get the position; after all, she was an outsider.

She had been driving about an hour now. The weather report said clear and sunny with a high of twenty below. How fast things changed around here, she mused. There were already four or five inches of snow covering the road, and it was still snowing. The road was a ribbon of pure white in the lights from the occasional oncoming cars as the inky blackness of night settled in. Gail was getting tired and tried again to think of something other than the job. It was no use. Memories once again flooded her mind.

She remembered that when she reached her job at the treatment centre her chest constricted, and the knot in the stomach felt like an anchor. Gail had moved from her community and left her support system of family, friends, and neighbours. There she had known only one person and that was only by sight. Others seemed cold and uncommunicative. She hadn't even started work and already she felt abandoned, isolated, and rejected. Those feelings never went away all the time she had worked there. In fact, they had bloomed like fireweed. She questioned herself time and time again. Had she made the biggest mistake of her life?

Gail knew something was wrong and questioned the treatment director about his treatment plan. Her apprehension mounted when she found his treatment plan had been nothing but exercise and diet. She was unsure about how her job was to fit in with the plan but didn't say anything to him. After all, he was the boss.

She remembered Donna, the Executive Director, as a powerful woman who had been constantly on the go. She knew how to talk with government officials and would not back down from anyone. Her enthusiasm for her work matched her ability to get the job done. She spoke her mind, and she had a clear, concise way of handling any obstacle to the construction and operation of the centre. Her ability had proven itself in the contributions she received from corporations and government officials for the construction, decoration, and operation of the centre. Gail liked her and trusted her.

Marvin, the treatment director was a man that some called a wimp. He had been working in different areas of the country and put himself on a pedestal. His underhandedness surpassed his arrogance. He constantly bragged about his having done all his healing through various methods, yet his comments and jokes always had a sleazy, sexual tone to them. Gail had avoided him and stayed in her office. Her work at first seemed to be shuffling papers from one side of the desktop to the other. Every time she asked Marvin a question, she got a different answer. She worked like that for a month, and the uneasiness climbed until one day she could take it no longer.

Either speak or leave, she said to herself. She knew that she had been looking for a job when she got that one. She had gone to Donna.

She thought of their conversation: "You know I think something is really wrong here. I'm not the treatment director, but I can't continue to work here if the treatment plan is nothing more than an exercise and diet program for alcoholics. They need more than that."

"So what's your idea of treatment," Donna asked, getting up and looking out the window at the construction of the new gym addition to the building.

"Well, treatment for any addicted person should, if possible, include: the twelve steps, cultural, and traditional components. Most importantly it should include healing the pains from the past which make people go out and drink or use in the first place – Adult Children of Trauma. You know the pain of growing up in trauma from being raised in an alcoholic or abusive home. Often people raised around alcoholism experience sexual abuse. Quite a few alcoholics and drug addicts are suffering from sexual abuse, and they need to deal with that. Also, an exercise plan of some sort and a meal plan for the whole centre that is going to promote abstinence should be included."

"Are you sure that there isn't something else behind this? I mean you and Marvin haven't exactly been the best of 'buddies' since you got here you know."

"My friendship, or lack thereof, has nothing to do with it. I just don't think that physical fitness and a drastic diet change are going to be the best treatment for everyone."

"Okay, I've been meaning to speak to Marvin about a few other things. I'll ask him what else he has in mind," Donna answered.

She had fired the treatment director a week later for conduct unbecoming to a professional. Donna didn't elaborate, but maybe others had complained about the sexual innuendos and the way he harassed the counsellors. The job of acting treatment director had been placed on Gail's shoulders. She was dumfounded. She had no idea that she would be expected to just jump in and develop a treatment program.

Gail remembered that the Executive Director had returned from a trip to Minnesota from another treatment centre and had handed her some papers. She said,

"Take an example from this treatment plan, add what you know and believe about treatment, add your training plan, and get this centre in operation. A trainer will be here in one week, and then you can take your staff to a centre for on-the-job training for two weeks."

Gail stood staring at her. Donna turned and walked back into her office, and Gail sat down. Minutes later she had picked up the telephone. She had set about calling the trainers she wanted to set up the training dates. She had cleared everything with the director and then got ready for the training that the Executive Director had set up.

She hadn't wanted to go to that training. She thought that she needed to be busy doing the paper work to set up the treatment plan. But Donna insisted. She insisted that Gail get the same training as the counsellors so she would know where they were and what more they may have needed. It was a good thing that Donna had insisted, Gail thought in retrospect.

Remembering the third day into the training, she sat with the staff and trainer in the talking circle, and shared her dreams. She told them about the dream she had before Marvin left work. She had seen many things at work, and had felt too intimidated to say anything. She had gone to bed and dreamt of being in a small rowboat on a really rough sea. The boat was tossing and turning and pieces of it were falling away as she helplessly sat there. She had written the dream down and went back to sleep. In the second dream, she was at a party where everyone but herself had been drinking. When it was time to leave, everyone had gotten on this bus. The bus driver asked her to drive because he was drunk. When she got the bus and passengers safely back to the station she she agreed to the job offer of assistant bus driver. She awakened from the dream, wrote the dream down, and again went back to sleep. It had been a powerful talking circle that morning.

She passed the eagle feather on to the next person on her left.

Joyce, the oldest woman on the counselling staff, had been very adamant about her traditional teachings. She stressed on a daily basis the importance of culture and traditions in the treatment program. She had taken the eagle feather and said, "I don't see why we have to do this training. We got all the training we needed during our first six weeks on the job, and I'm not going to write no test. I don't need no certificate to say what I know. I'm gonna do what I want when we get them clients." She had turned and quickly passed the eagle feather on.

George was sitting next to Joyce. He stated he was not going to go away on the trip. "I figure I can do on-the-job training here at this treatment centre. I know that I am ready to help the clients when they come in." He handed the eagle feather to Marlin.

Marlin was a beautiful lady who learned to speak English by reading the Big Book of Alcoholics Anonymous and had received help from her A.A. sponsor. She had given her name, said she was feeling good, and then passed the feather to Derek.

The eagle feather had gone around and finally the last two spoke.

Debra, a tall, thin young woman, spoke quietly.

"I may not know all I need to know of my traditional ways, but I do know that I can help my people. I too have taken the cultural training we need to run this treatment centre. I am interested in this training. I know we are going to have a traditional-cultural treatment centre, and it wouldn't hurt to learn about other stuff."

Beth, a tiny, gentle lady, not much older than Gail was the last to speak.

"I may know some of the teachings, but I don't brag about what I know. Gail, you are the new treatment director and I'm here to be a counsellor. I will follow your directions because you are my boss. I will take this training, and I will do my best. I will also take the other training you offer. I wanna keep learning."

Gail returned to her office at the end of the talking circle. She had had enough. She didn't have a chance to call her friend for support because Donna knocked on the door and walked in at that moment. Donna invited her to accompany her on some errands and to have lunch in town. She wanted to talk about the treatment plan and the training.

Gail remembered having been half reluctant to go and half glad for the break. She grabbed her coat and purse and followed Donna out the door. Once in the car, she sighed and relaxed a little. She had more than ever felt like a failure that day, having heard all the negativity at the talking circle.

Donna had driven around doing her errands and asked about the training. Gail told her that it was frustrating and that the counsellors were "getting to know each other." Donna was upset with that. She told her that they had been in training for six weeks and had plenty of opportunity to get to know each other.

Remembering that day, she questioned Donna about the previous training. It had been six weeks of cultural and traditional training. They had six weeks of training but nothing about alcoholism and drug abuse. She wondered how they would have allowed that kind of training, and Donna informed her that the trainer had been related to a board member. Donna said, "You also have to remember that most of the Board of Directors know nothing about treatment. Some are just learning about their culture, and there are only one or two that are sober. I mean really sober."

Gail remembered her surprise at that statement. "So, the board members are not clean and sober, and the counsellors were taught culture in a classroom?" she had said. "Were they gonna have exams too? I see that they have big notebooks and lots of handouts. I got a copy from Debra. She seems to follow Joyce all over the place, and she was happy to share her notes with me."

Culture had been the main focus of the treatment program before Gail had gone to work there, and then she changed things. She remembered the uneasy feeling she had with the staff taking sides. On one side were the counsellors and staff who wanted it the old way, and on the other, staff and counsellors who supported Gail and her development of the new treatment plan. She tried so hard to make the staff see that she wasn't taking away from their old ideas; she had only added new ideas. She told them, "We all need to know everything we can about alcoholism and drug abuse treatment. You are all strong in your culture, and that will help a lot. Please listen with an open mind to other trainers, other ideas, and most of all to each other. The client must come first."

She continuously felt responsible for the staff. She felt anxious when someone seemed unhappy, and she held in her anger when she felt that things were not going right. She felt that it wasn't safe to talk to anyone.

That first year, the treatment program had been successful. There were four groups of clients that graduated before the end of July. Of the previous graduates, thirty in all, all but one stayed sober. The staff was elated. They worked hard and some counsellors had excitedly talked about more training. Other staff members talked of more treatment tools and the work they could do when they came back in the fall after their well-deserved break.

She remembered in that new year that the treatment centre operated regularly for the first six weeks. The staff received more training at the end of the vacation and were ready to begin their work. Then the inevitable happened. The two male staff members quit. The availability of healthy, male treatment counsellors had been nonexistent. It had been a treatment centre operating understaffed, and the staff that worked there were under stress.

Late in November, Gail felt that the end had come. Disillusioned, she continued to throw herself into her work. There had been a division in the centre for months around the treatment plan and styles, and it continued to widen. There were staff who had constantly berated the treatment plan to the board and, the community members, and a meeting was called to decide what to do with the treatment centre.

Letting those memories drift away, she drove through the deep snow on the road with the darkness settling in. The heavy snowfall was now a blizzard, and Gail's fear turned into terror as she clutched the steering wheel. Her eagle feather sat on her pillow next to her. She reached down and grabbed it. Gail kept praying to the Creator for help. Then, her thoughts would drift again.

She remembered the community meeting. Gail had listened to the words from all who spoke. There had been supportive words for the staff and the treatment centre. Then, the words from the staff wanting changes cut through her like a knife. She left. Her hopes dashed. The end had come. She had worked so hard, and they still hadn't heard. She had seen that the counsellors who wanted only sweat lodges and talking circles won. She had known deep in her heart that no matter what she said, they would not take directions from her.

The end of the meeting brought resolution to most of the problems. She should have been happy. The treatment centre got full support from the bands and the community members. Why then did Gail have the sinking feeling?

She returned from Christmas holidays with renewed vigor and enthusiasm. She felt ready to fight tooth and nail for what she believed to be a good treatment plan, but her resolve had ended at the second week in January. Although the community had spoken of support, the board and some staff continued operating on the premise that they would have only sweat lodges and talking circles. The two counsellors that continued the treatment program, as she designed it, had gotten tired. Staff members called in sick and started looking for other jobs. She had been unable to fight, and she hadn't even been able stay at work. Tears came to her eyes, and she wept at her desk.

Gail called her friend in Montana and sobbed into the phone. "I'm so tired; I don't want to do this anymore."

Her friend listened to her and then said, "Go to the doctor. Tell him how you feel and maybe he can give you a doctor's note prescribing time off for a rest."

Taking her friend's advice, she called her doctor and made the appointment. Gail had gone to the Executive Director and told her she was sick. She left the office and walked out the door.

Now, here she was, driving in a blinding snow storm.

"God, please help. You drive 'cause I can't see and I'm scared." She pushed forward through the wall of white, clutching the eagle feather. Then, realizing that the Creator had been helping, she settled back against the car seat. She had come through some traumatic things these past two years with the help of the Creator, and she knew that she would get through this.

The frigid lake, wild and furious, was on the left. A sheer mountain was on the right. The road curved in a snake's path. Meeting a car anywhere right then might mean she'd become part of the scenery. Her hands rested on the steering wheel in a gentle but firm grasp instead of the clutching she had been doing for the past two hours. She survived the ordeal at the treatment centre. Her sickness that she had imagined as some terrible disease was only Post Traumatic Stress Disorder treatable by rest, food, and fresh air. And now she felt confident that she would survive this drive and whatever else was placed in front of her.

Abruptly, the snow became like feathers falling from a broken pillow. Gail settled back and relaxed. She thanked the Creator as she sighed a breath of relief. The last two hours of driving seemed like all she could take; and the memories came again.

Gail cleaned out her desk. She told the Executive Director she needed six weeks off, but she knew she wouldn't return.

Now, as she drove, she thought of all that she had come through. The last two hours seemed like the end of a big test. Suddenly the lights went out. There was a slight "click" sound and nothing. Absolutely nothing. After a few minutes to adjust her eyes, unable to stop because of the treacherous condition of the roads, she could see. No headlights, no dash lights, nothing was visible but a ribbon of white in front of the slow, steady movement of her car.

She grabbed the CB sitting there beside her and called out for help. There was no response. No one was listening that she could see or hear. Gail shut off the CB and said

"Okay, Creator, if you are listening I have another request. I need you to drive again because I really can't see now without lights, or else turn on the lights." The lights came back on. Had this been another test? All the things she had just been through – working, driving in this storm, and now the lights – were they a test just to see if she really relied on the Creator or believed in him?

Her sigh of relief sounded like the wind in a tunnel. Her perilous journey seemed to be coming to an end. The job was miles behind her and the road ahead was clear.

Gail drove another twenty minutes and found a motel that was open with a vacancy. She had been on the road only six hours since her supper break, but it seemed like twenty. As she settled into bed after a hot bath and a meal, she let her mind drift. Where would the next "test" take her? She had been through so much. This last job was not the only struggle she had. She remembered her recovery from the sexual abuse traumas, the training and counselling sessions. Her education in the large university, where they could care less if you were Indian and what your needs were. All these different things she had come through. It was all worth it though she was so tired. As she drifted into sleep, she gave thanks and asked for guidance for her next journey.

11

CO-DEPENDENCE: THE ETERNAL VICTIM

C o-dependence is debilitating to many people and yet they may not even realize that they have this malady. Co-dependence is a disease of the inner child/spirit or the lost self. It is associated with, or can aggravate, and even lead to many physical, mental, emotional or spiritual problems that occur in daily life.

We become co-dependent when we turn our responsibility for our life and happiness over to other people and to what some therapists call our false self. We focus outwardly on other people and their happiness or wellness instead of looking in at ourselves. The lost or false self is the person we became when we were not sure what role we were supposed to be playing in childhood. We wanted so much for everything to be "okay" or "better." We turned ourselves into pretzels trying to make things better so Mom or Dad wouldn't drink or so the abuse would stop. Our inner child, the real spiritual, creative, fun-loving person, goes into hiding.

As adults and for some, even earlier in life, co-dependents become so preoccupied with others that they neglect themselves, who they really are, the spirit within. Underneath the hard, controlling, super-responsible mom may be the wonderful, funny, loving, creative woman buried as a child.

We describe any suffering or dysfunction that is associated with or results from focusing on the needs and behaviours of others as co-dependence. A typical symptom of co-dependence is martyrdom, someone who is constantly doing, and constantly complaining or talking about their hard work.

Co-dependence is the most common of all addictions – the addiction of looking elsewhere. We believe that something outside ourselves can give us happiness and fulfillment. The "elsewhere" may be people, places, things, behaviours, or experiences, e.g. the next drink, the chocolate bar, the ice cream, the next man/woman fantasy life, winning the next big game or the next big promotion, the bingo game, the lottery.

Self-neglect alone is no fun. The payoff for the co-dependent comes from focusing outward. The payoff is that the more time we spend on focusing out, the less time we have to spend looking within. It may be too painful to look inside. It is much easier to look out there, and see how I can make my daughter have a better life, for example. How can I help her make the "right" choices in school, career or relationships?

We learn co-dependence from others around us which makes it not only an addiction but a contagious or acquired illness. From the time we are born, we see co-dependent behaviour modeled and taught by a string of important people: parents, teachers, siblings, friends. Even watching TV (soap operas) and movies, we learn co-dependence. Media, government, and organized religion that teaches you "don't be selfish – do for others" and the helping profession also reinforce co-dependent behaviour.

Co-dependence is a result of trying to protect our delicate child within, the spirit memory of what you were like as a baby from what are overwhelming forces outside ourselves. The child within is not only sensitive and vulnerable, but it is also powerful. When our alive, inner child goes into hiding to survive, a false, co-dependent self emerges to takes its place. A false self emerges to please the parents and other adult figures. Fear is a tremendous motivator.

We lose our awareness of ourselves to such an extent that we lose awareness of the existence of that inner child. We lose contact with who we are; we begin to think we are the false self so that it becomes a habit and finally an addiction. We do not become aware of the child within until, as with other addictions, "we hit bottom."

We describe co-dependence not only as the most common addiction, but as the basis for all other addictions and compulsions. When we've experienced shame-based trauma in our lives as children, and we feel we are somehow defective, we mix that with the drive of that child to be strong and self-expressive. We set ourselves up for the addictive, compulsive behaviour of co-dependence, a disorder that makes us believe that only something outside us can make us happy and fulfilled.

Women in our society are socialized to feel satisfaction and fulfillment only from meeting the needs of others, by putting others first in their lives. Women learn to center their lives around the needs of partners, spouses, children, or aged parents at the expense of their own lives. They are unable to set limits because they fear abandonment.

We now have just as many men in the same situation as women. How many men do you know who are working themselves to death for the next big promotion? Trying to please that boss? Still trying to make it better for the little kid inside?

Indigenous people come from a tradition of extended families and before Christianity so did other nations. We lived in communities and always had the elders living within the family until they chose to move on to the other world. In our extended family society, before the coming of the Europeans, we lived together and worked together. We didn't segregate elders into nursing homes or farm children out to strangers. Communal living meant communal support for all ages. The extended families took care of each other. Everyone was responsible and cared for each other's children. Everyone was responsible and took care of the elderly. They were not placed in old-age homes, and there was never a need for orphanages and foster homes. The women all worked together. The men were involved as well. It was a natural part of the world they lived in.

Today we have the elderly being placed in nursing homes because their children are career people and have jobs. We have day care to look after the children because both parents need to work to provide all that the family wants. People are working hard in life to earn the money to live the life that we "are supposed to live." This is how society promotes co-dependency. To have all the appliances, the cars, the boats, the ski packages, and the big fancy houses many people work themselves to death. "We must do this in order for our children to have such and such." Everyone is not trying to "keep up with the Jones." They are all the Jones. The poor and lower middle class are becoming more disgruntled and co-dependent themselves trying to keep up with the rest of the world.

Often we misconstrue the roles of the traditional families. When a grandparent has the young children living with them – to the detriment of their own health, I would ask is that traditional or is it co-dependence? Is it traditional to enable parents to squander money on booze and bingo while the grandparents use their pension cheque to try to provide a healthy home for the children?

How do we separate ourselves from the problems and provide an opportunity for the children and grandchildren to have healthy lives? When do we say no? What is enabling and what is caring? When do we stop putting the rest of the world first and begin to care for ourselves as individuals and as a community? The church teaches that to do for ourselves is being selfish. It teaches that to be selfish is a sin. I maintain that looking after ourselves is not selfish. It is not sinful to say I need a break. To say to someone who asks for your help, "I will be much stronger and able to help you if I take a rest or if I take the time for myself." It is not selfish to say, "No I can't babysit tonight. I need to sleep so that I will be refreshed when I am asked to help tomorrow."

Look within. Are you taking care of yourself? Or are you putting everyone else first and wearing yourself out? Are you becoming ill? Are you run down from caring for everyone but yourself? Are you putting the booze and the gambling on the same level as the children?

I saw a little four-year-old girl in a large shopping area in one of those big box stores; she was crying so hard she could hardly see. She was not lost. She was crying because she could not get her two or three-year-old brother to stop looking at things and go with her to find her mom. I wondered when did her responsibility for her little brother set in? When did she take over the role of that mother to care for a child in such a huge place? How many other times has she had to be the mom? How long will she carry that role? I did say that older children were shown how to care for younger ones and were allowed to help. The operative words here are "older children were shown."

Little children learned to play and be children. When they asked to help they were encouraged and "shown how" to do things. They were not given total responsibility for the safety and well-being of younger siblings. I wonder if the little girl in the shopping warehouse will ever find her true self? Will she forever be looking after others? Will she spend her whole life trying to get others to listen to her and make them do things? How many other people, who are bosses that are controlling and constantly trying to fix things for everyone, are products of that kind of experience in childhood? I know I was. I tried my utmost in a job to make things better for everyone. I tried to be everything for everyone to the detriment of my health. I was diagnosed with Post Traumatic Stress Disorder. I burned out from being co-dependent. I found myself in a situation similar to my childhood where I paid more attention to the people and the situations at the workplace than I did to myself.

When we focus so much outside ourselves, we lose touch with what is inside. We lose touch with our beliefs and our thoughts and feelings. We do not make decisions or choices for ourselves. Our other experiences, wants, and needs are put aside. We disregard the sensations, intuitions, unconscious experiences, and even indicators of our physical functioning such as heart rate and respiratory rate. It is up to me to take the time to look after myself. If I put myself and my health and well-being first now, then I am better able to be there for my family, friends, and job/career later.

We will no longer need to focus outside and watch everyone else's business. We no longer need to go to bars, bingos, casinos etc. to try and fix what is missing in our lives. We can rest when we are tired, and can say no to something that is unhealthy for us. We no longer need to work eighteen hours a day to make the bosses happy so that we may keep our jobs. We recognize the same symptoms of Post Traumatic Stress Disorder (PTSD) that we get now and again when we are doing too much for others and not enough for ourselves. We have to be vigilant in our everyday lives to look after ourselves physically so that we don't get too hungry, angry, lonely, or tired or we may end up relapsing into our disease of co-dependency and/or addictions.

I have found that there are other jobs available that I enjoy, and that when I enjoy my work I am healthier and happier inside. If I am working too hard, I only hurt myself. The company always appreciates someone who will work themselves to the bone. It is better for them. The employee suffers and the company expands. Today I do what I can, and the rest will wait for tomorrow. If I drop dead today, the boss will hire someone else and the job will get done without me anyway. I don't need to kill myself.

Co-dependency is a disease/addiction/compulsion that is fear based. Fear of abandonment, fear of failure, fear of fear. It seems that anything that can make that fear feeling go away will be okay for now. We think, "Anything that I can do to make you happy makes me happy." But does it? Are you looking after people in your life because you are truly happy inside? Or are you doing it because you "are supposed to?" Are you afraid that they won't love you or that they will leave you? Are you caring for your grandchildren to the detriment of your health and, in turn, being crabby and emotionally unavailable for them? Is that what you really wanted to give to your grandchildren?

Are you putting in long hours at a job that you don't really enjoy because you are afraid that you can't get that next item you wanted to buy for your partner or child? Saying no to your boss for overtime or extra work could change things for you. Maybe the boss will see a person of great merit who she/he can rely on for a more prestigious job that doesn't require overtime. And just maybe that extra time spent with family is what they really wanted in the first place and not the expensive toys you buy because you feel guilty.

Co-dependence is an internal struggle. Only you can decide if you are taking care of yourself and your inner child. Only you can decide what is right for you.

I have learned that one of the best support groups for co-dependents besides

Co-dependence Anonymous is the Al-Anon program. It is also a 12-step program. It teaches you to, very simply, let go and let God take care of things.

I Remember

> she knelt on the floor,
> felt the collision of knees against wood
> the smell of the new pine lumber
> leading to the image of forests
> dark, foreboding, silent
> where she sat as a child many times in trees
> back against the heart surrounded in arms strong,
> sturdy,
> that held and comforted her
> hiding from the pain
> of rejection, abandonment,
> dreaming of the safety and love in another world so
> distant and foreign
> a taste of metal in her mouth
> the nails were sharp, tangy, salty,
> a razor-sharp pain as she took each nail
> one at a time
> placed it on the floor and hit it a resounding thud
> with each bang of the hammer her pain and hurt,
> nailed solid within her breast
> her anger and hate fastened under the slats
> of her rib cage
> along with the thrust of her anger
> she pounded out the fury of loneliness
> she needed to be accepted,
> like her brothers

the sound of their laughter – teasing, hurting,
drowned her thoughts
the tears welled in her eyes
determination and pride kept them from dropping
to the new floor
she kept her head bent
watching the men and seeing
with eyes that needed to be washed with tears
the wide gap in gender and connection
she focused intently on the job ahead
out of the corner of her eye
she saw different shades of brown hazing into a blur
the copper brown of her father's weather-beaten face
the dark golden browns of her brothers' faces
the rich chocolate amber brown of the beer bottles
as they sat amidst tools
needed for the job
the colours melded together into a bubbling, frothing,
liquid
as her eyes brimmed over and
once more she lowered her head to the task at hand
her cracked and drying hands reached
to brush away a tear and again to wipe her brow
she mentions the heat
and the sweat that gets in the eyes
they make no comment as if she isn't there
she is invisible
she continues pounding, nailing,
wishing
to belong
to be accepted to be loved
her pain is pushed aside her heart nailed shut
swimming in the amber liquid

she joined the men and swallowed hard the ache of
loneliness
she moved and left the roof to stand beside a man
much like her father and brothers
his laughter hid the pain,
and the dark rich chocolate amber brown
of the beer bottles needed
to finish jobs
started and couldn't finish
she continued to hold the hammer
bite the nails she held in her mouth
to fix and mend the broken home
he was a politician a man with humor,
his laughter held hurt, scars, and blocked tears
she nailed the floor she walked
in deadened silence
her tools a choice of liquid in brown glass
that washed away the rust
surrounding the place that once was her heart
again she is alone
he chose to drink the amber liquid
wash away their love in silence
his jokes had caused laughter
now silenced
they carry him one last time
to his place of rest beside his father
his brother and mother
the brown chocolate amber of the bottles
sit alone in testimony
of his existence
she walks alone and looks upon the family she has to
raise
the son and daughter who bring her joy

and laughter that has no edge
a smooth and rounded love
acceptance of mistakes
and the growing she has done along with them
her son is grown
his famous roles
his childhood jungle book life is now on stage
he laughs with joy and cries his pain
and he looks with gratitude at life to explore
she taught him well
now years later she stands alone
and brushes away a tear no longer hiding
no longer bowing her head in pain
the drying and cracking now describes her insides
the pounding of her heart now nails love for her
daughter
as she sheds tears of sadness and releases her child
her daughter of twenty now leaving their home,
her child venturing out not herself,
her daughter
a confident young woman
who doesn't need to kneel beside her brother
to feel accepted, wanted, loved
she walks away to join her friends
and becomes the adventurer she wants to be
the woman knows the pain of mothers
she feels the pain
yet she can watch her daughter walk away
her head held high
she knows the love she gave that child is what she
worked for
kneeling, nailing, crying, seeing,
so long ago
Barbara-Helen Hill 1995

12

TELLING SECRETS

One of the hardest steps in recovery is to tell one's secrets. To look into the past and explore all the painful memories, and circumstances and bring them into the open can be extremely difficult. But recovery must also be emotional healing. It is not enough to just talk about painful memories. We need to look at the memories, deal with the emotions attached to those memories, and release the pain.

Shame is one layer of healing that we have to look at. Men have always been more highly valued in most, if not all, societies so simply being a woman can be the beginning of shame. We as Native people have learned to feel that there is something inadequate about us; something that cannot be fixed. And around this core of shame, we have built our identities.

Shame now exists independently in our psyches, and we carry those feelings with us wherever we go. Internal or external experiences can trigger these shameful feelings.

Ongoing recovery is about empowerment – the ability to feel power and take action. Healing our sense of shame is the basis of our empowerment. Shame immobilizes and takes away our power. You feel you have no energy, no hope, and no sense of the possibility of movement. Shame becomes a vicious cycle. The more shame you feel, the more initiative you lose. Going within yourself to look at your childhood abuse, your trauma, or your source of shame is the first step toward becoming assertive.

Sources of shame in our society includes race, ethnicity, cultural orientation, education, income, and sexual preference. If you stop and look at it, these are just a part of the variety of ways of being that gives life its rich complexity. If you can get in touch with your wise, inner self, you will know that there is no shame or glory attached to any of it. You are just who you are. There is no easy cure or quick fix. Therapy can help you restore a healthy process of dealing with life instead of acting from shame, but effecting such a change takes time.

During healing you will often re-experience those deep feelings of shame that you built up and could not control which often translates as compulsive behaviour, e.g. alcohol/drug abuse, compulsive eating, and other eating disorders. As you work through the feelings with the help of therapy and support groups, you will find new behavioral patterns and find yourself feeling extremely vulnerable at times.

Part of your recovery will find you moving into a healthier way of creating a sense of personal sexual dignity. You will find self-empowerment and act on your sexuality on your own behalf without violating or coercing others. You will become accountable for your sexual self as well as your recovery. Working through issues that have kept you from your self-empowerment, from taking responsibility for learned patterns such as helplessness, guilt, sexual abuse, and shame provides healing. This recovery will enable you to have intimacy with yourself and with those you love.

To begin recovery and heal the shame and guilt from the abuse and traumas we experienced as children, we need to choose to give up the alcohol/drug abuse or any other addictive, compulsive cover-up techniques. When we give up an abusive relationship, we take the time to nurture ourselves. We give up the destructive relationship and the fear that we will never find another person. After shedding these, we can become open to the attention of someone we had not even noticed.

Through healing, we go through a period of grieving and remorse. We even mourn the loss of our addictive or compulsive substances. Addicts find it difficult to give up their attachments because they chose to give themselves completely to alcohol, food, gambling, drugs, work, sex, relationships, and/or a quest of power no matter how self-destructive it was.

Because of the trauma and our fear of more trauma, we kept quiet. We had no one to trust, no one to talk to. We must learn to break the silence, and let the secrets come out into the light. "We are only as sick as our secrets." Our families may balk. Yet if we continue to keep silent, we are not only denying our own health but we are also denying the opportunity for our families to get well.

If we were sexually abused, our abusers have coerced us into keeping silent, if not by threats of physical damage to ourselves, then perhaps by threats to our loved ones. They may have told us we would be sent away. We might also have the underlying feeling that we won't be believed. I know in my childhood I took on the blame and felt that if I told anyone, they would think that it was my fault. Sometimes we have this idea that we don't want to hurt someone else. We kept silent, thinking, "Mom or Dad would be so hurt if they found out that she/he did that to me." Often, they threatened the abuse of our siblings, or the murder of us or other members of the family.

> *"The reasons we learn to keep the secret control our lives as much as the abuse. If we believe in telling others what happened to us, that we will be sent away or won't be believed, our entire lives will be controlled by the fear of getting too close to people for fear of being sent away or not believed."* (Kellogg & Harrison 1991:131)

Many things prevent us from telling. The individual needs to feel safe to help the inner child reveal the secret or secrets and work through the trauma. In recovery we face those fears. We work through them and face not only the fears of abandonment but the fears of walking through the memories. Telling the secrets where it is safe allows us to reclaim ourselves, our spirits, and to discover we are no longer alone. Then, we are on the road to recovery.

13

SEXUALITY & SPIRITUALITY

I t has always been my theory that sexuality is about who you are – your feelings, emotions and boundaries. We each need to define our identity to let someone else get to know us, by defining our role as a friend, lover, partner, and as a positive role model to children.

In a healthy relationship, sex is the ultimate joy and the ultimate way of showing your love. I don't see a relationship lasting if all you have is just a physical interaction. A relationship needs to be mutually respectful and fulfilling in all areas. If you are being true to yourself, you will set the boundaries and state what is good for you. If the person you are interacting with cannot understand your need to look after yourself then maybe you should look at that. Are they using you for their own satisfaction without regard for you? Are you or they using sex as a weapon?

We need to be able to say what we like and do not like, what we will and will not accept. We need to be in touch with our sexual feelings, also other feelings and emotions and to express them freely. Sexuality is knowing who you are as a woman or a man physically, emotionally, spiritually, and mentally. Finding out who we are and allowing conversations to come from the love in the heart, not from an angry place, is essential as well as liberating.

In our extended families, before colonization, we learned healthy sexual patterns from our parents and from the interaction among all of our other relations. Colonization altered the flow of the extended families and clan systems as they originally were. Our families became nuclear families which eventually became fractionalized and dysfunctional. Our sexual teachings went out the window, or should I say they became the focus of television programs. Sex was no longer a sacred spiritual emotional gift to yourself and your partner. Sex became the focus for ad campaigns. Suddenly we saw sex for sale, as a marketable commodity. Men and women began to objectify each other. As sex became confused, respect for self and each other was lost.

With colonization and "churchianity," we stopped talking about sex. Parents listened to the church injected doctrines of the Puritans and sex became a taboo subject for discussion. The church spoke often of the sins of sex and the sins of the woman temptress. Respect for women was lost, and with that loss, came the loss of the natural teachings.

Healthy sexuality is not taught the way other subjects are taught in school. It is learned from your parents, and other role models in your community. Males learn healthy sexuality from watching men and from interacting with women – their mothers, aunts, and grandmothers, also siblings and female friends. Females learn the same way. They emulate their moms, aunties and grandmothers. They interact with their fathers and other males in the community, thus getting a reflection of their male side. They learn that they can do things; they have a healthy reflection from the healthy males and thus they become balanced.

With colonization and the puritanical teachings of the church came the lack of respect. With the lack of respect came the shame. Suddenly it was taboo to speak of sex and anyone who asked questions was shushed. The lack of teachings about sexuality mixed with the other results of colonialism, such as the alcohol abuse and the lack of parenting skills, resulted in substantial amounts of sexual abuse. When you are not taught, and you feel shame for even thinking about sex, you feel that shame to your very core. As a result, you have dysfunctional sexual behaviour that often translates into abuse. If sexuality is who we are as humans, and if we are to recognize it is part of our spirituality, then any type of abuse to our human psyche results not only in sexual abuse but also in spiritual abuse.

It is no wonder that we as humans currently question where it will all end. There are many forms of abuse around the world today. Healthy sexuality and healthy responsible love are not topics for television. The topic must be marketable. Health does not seem to sell these days.

I watched Oprah for about ten minutes one day. A woman stood up in the audience and spoke of how she was a person who left clothes lying around in her apartment for two weeks. She let dishes pile up in the sink and ate too much too often. She was not saying something was wrong; on the contrary she thought she was okay. She didn't see that she had a problem. Granted, maybe she doesn't. If you like living like that, and are content with your life and don't question anything, maybe you are okay. When you have compulsions or addictions and you start questioning yourself and your way of life, there is not only the recognition of a possible problem but the beginnings of looking at a solution.

Puritanical thinking and colonialism created confusion around sex and love when the Europeans came into the Native communities. Sex expresses love. To know and respect oneself as a man or woman allows us to better express one's sexuality. How one relates to others expresses who we are. If one has low self-worth and self-esteem, it shows in the way she/he relates sexually to others. If one does not love oneself, one cannot love someone else or believe that others love him/her.

Not all difficulties in a person's life are the result of sexual abuse as we have known it. Not all abuse is fondling, touching, oral or anal intercourse. The lack of sex education, the lack of healthy responsible role models can also be abusive. If in any way you feel ashamed about any part of your life, maybe there is where you need to look.

Sexual recovery is understanding the relationship between sexuality and spirituality and knowing about our bodies. Getting counselling and support can help us to learn to like our bodies as they are and to have same sex friends. It is learning to enjoy sexual feelings, develop boundaries, and to enjoy ourselves sexually. It is learning to say no and that we can change our minds any time. Sexual recovery allows us to talk about sex, to learn about the difference between safe sex, addictive sex, abusive sex, and healthy sex. It is okay to flirt and learn to enjoy healthy seduction. Sexual recovery takes time, and patience. It is also well worth the effort that the abused and their partner will see with proper help and guidance.

It is okay to question yourself. It is okay to seek help if you are dissatisfied with your life. The only stupid question is the one un-asked. How do we go about reaching each other today? How do we teach our children and let them know that it is okay to have diverse sexual feelings? If they have not seen you act responsibly as parents, they are certain to be embarrassed for you if you try to express your concern.

It is my contention that it is never too late for anyone to change. If our children learn more by watching, then I believe it is most important for us as adults, parents, and even grandparents to start modeling healthy lifestyles. That way there will at least be a child somewhere who will grow up to have some semblance of a healthy life. Somewhere out there, there will be one less abused child in the next generation and one less abuser walking around the streets preying upon an innocent victim.

We are not always talking about sex when we speak of love. I connect love with the Creator, with creativity, with sexuality. I view sex as an expression of that love when the time and the relationship is right. After speaking to a few couples, I have heard that the best love that they have felt and the best sexual experience that they have had is when they have fallen in love with their best friend.

Condolence
A Time of Healing

You have walked many miles
and your journey has been rough
Sit, rest awhile
let us wash your face and hands with cedar water
to remove the pain and debris
that has attached itself
to you on your many days of travel
Rest your back against the pine
as we bathe your feet and legs in cedar water
to remove the briars
you have collected from your long walk
Let us brush your hair
remove the tangles, and burs,
release the confusion from your mind
Let go of your troublesome worries
Drink this clear cool water as it springs forth
from earth's breast to quench your thirst
and wet your parched throat that your words
may be clear and you may speak the truth
We will wipe your eyes
with the soft skin of a fawn
remove the pain you carry
from the sights along your journey
so that you will again see with clarity
the beauty of life that abounds
We will wipe your ears
with the soft down of the eagle feather
to remove the blocks from your ears
that you may hear with clarity
the sounds of life that abound
Rest and let us bring you some soup made with corn

from the corn mother and her sisters, beans and squash
We will feed you that you will nourish your body
and you will rest to join our circle in
Thanksgiving that you have arrived
and you are welcomed to sit with us in wellness
and we will sing together the songs of life.
Barbara-Helen Hill 1996

14

RE-EVALUATION COUNSELLING

"In 1950, a man by the name of Harvey Jackins, in Seattle, Washington, developed, expanded, and improved a system for people to relate to each other in a helpful manner. They named this system of helping 'Re-evaluation Counselling.' Since 1970, this technique or style of counselling has spread throughout the United States into Canada and about thirty-eight other countries.

Individuals learn about Re-evaluation Counselling through their attendance and participation in co-counselling 'communities. 'They are basically support groups similar to Alcoholics Anonymous (A.A.) or Adult Children of Alcoholics (A.C.O.A.) groups; through workshops, seminars, and lectures, or through exploring the literature on the subject. There is no formal school of learning that an individual attends and becomes certified.

Re-evaluation Counselling was developed as a system to help individuals from all walks of life and occupations and from every cultural and ethnic background. It could be used and adapted to their particular field. Many elementary school teachers in the United States have used the counselling techniques to help them change difficult situations within the classroom. These teachers have used the ideas of validation

and support in working with children." (Diane Hill at a
workshop in Thunder Bay, Ontario. 1989)

I n 1984 I became associated with Tribal Sovereignty Associates,
Bob Antone and Diane Hill, and they introduced me to the "Re-
evaluation Co-counselling" process. They had been working
both in Canada and in the United States on developing a counselling
process for Native people. Their counselling techniques have encouraged individuals in communities as well as whole groups of community members to start their healing. With their help, I began in earnest
my healing that had started five years before in Al-Anon.

They started working with this type of counselling in 1983. Their
counselling process and training have helped many Native people including myself. Learning their process marked the beginning of my
healing. Their belief, and mine, is that the healing of the spirit is an
important process for individual growth and personal development.
The counselling process as explained by Diane and Bob is a way to
"empower" the individual with a higher sense of self-confidence, self-
worth, and self-esteem.

The basis for the counselling process is listening to people. Really
listening. Often when people gather there are people talking, and
there are people listening. In reality, the people listening are also
thinking about other things such as what they are going to say. They
may even be wishing that the person talking would shut up so they
can talk. In the co-counselling process developed, people take turns
paying attention (full attention) to each other. They take turns talking about themselves and then listening to the other person. This
process of sharing is important and has great effects on a sense of
wellbeing.

Listening and, most importantly, paying attention to another person is the basis of how we approach co-counselling. The counselling
process begins with the assumption that all human beings are naturally wholesome and good. It also supports the assumption that human beings possess great intelligence with the ability to think and

create new responses to every new situation we face – the ability to think clearly, rationally, and logically. When humans are free of distress, they possess the ability to operate rationally and logically. They will always create something new to suit any situation.

Humans have a process of sorting out and thinking through a situation. We call this process "evaluation," evaluating the information and then choosing the best response to the situation. During the evaluation process, we are using our intelligence. We are using our ability to think clearly and logically. We think with our minds and hearts connected.

Stress, emotional pain, or for that matter any pain impairs the ability to think clearly and logically. Any emotional or physical hurt interrupts our ability to think clearly and logically; our ability to come up with new answers and solutions to problems becomes impaired.

The Tribal Sovereignty Associates approach explained that painful or stressful experience causes the human to be unable to evaluate clearly the information coming at them. Unevaluated information from a hurtful experience doesn't go away. It becomes stored within the human and acts like a recording of what went on during bad times. We might remember the sounds, the smells, the tastes. We also remember the people in the vicinity, how we felt, how we acted, or in some cases, how we simply ignored what was happening. We shut down our thinking in order to cope. Our recorder remembers, somewhere deep in the physical memory and the subconscious, what we did to survive the trauma.

Any time a new experience resembles a past stressful experience, the recording within us will come on automatically. We find ourselves acting or reacting to stress in a specific pattern that is usually rigid and uncomfortable. Most often we are unaware that we are acting in a behavioral pattern. In addiction we use the act of reaching for a drink, or using food or drugs as a method of coping or responding to a situation. This then can become a pattern – a rigid form of behaviour. In some experiences we might find ourselves shutting down our thinking because the particular situation reminds us of something from the past. Because we fail to evaluate information, we develop a pattern of ignoring, or of running away, from an upsetting situation.

We need to re-evaluate painful experiences and find out what hold it might have on our thinking. Underneath the pain is the ability to create, and to be a human capable of loving the self and other human beings.

In co-counselling, we listen and pay attention to the person. We provide the opportunity for the person to visit and speak about their painful experience. The person then releases or discharges any painful feelings. Feelings not released trap the ability to think clearly and act lovingly towards others. We listen to that person without judgment and without blame. We know that underneath the pattern there is a good and loving human being. Upon evaluation, the individual and the counsellor find that the individual has done the very best that they could at the time and deserves no blame or reproach from anyone, including themselves.

In a work situation, I was forever being confronted by an over sized woman who constantly argued and belittled me at every turn. I kept trying to think of the positive and kept trying to be firm in my position but was constantly a basket case emotionally when I went home at night. With a bit of counselling from Bob I could see that the woman, although very helpful in some ways, was constantly "pushing my buttons." What we found was that this woman constantly reminded me of an aunt. This aunt would always find fault with me and my behaviour and constantly compared me to her daughter. I was always trying to be something that I wasn't because I couldn't meet *"her"* standards.

Counselling helped me to tell my aunt, who is long deceased, to "fluffle up a gum tree" and that I was okay the way I was. I didn't need to do things differently to please her. I was doing what was right for me. After that session, I saw my co-worker for who she was and not as my aunt. I could stand firmly in my position and could do my job to the best of my ability.

We support the individual by giving them kindness, encouragement, warmth, and the love of one human to another just as the Creator loves. We support them to release their feelings by crying, trembling, yawning, laughing (in many forms), by angry shouting, or in some cases repetitive or eager talk. Any type of discharge or release of distress frees the original, functioning, good-natured human inside.

The release of the pain allows the person to re-evaluate the situation and feel empowered with new knowledge and new energy for moving on in their daily life. Co-counselling has allowed many individuals to understand their particular behaviour through finding the source of their painful experiences and re-evaluating their information. New and supportive behaviours replace old and inappropriate behaviours. Feeling good about the self replaces feeling bad. Thinking has become clearer, and we make choices with greater awareness.

Eruption

> Mountains erupt from my breast
> dark jagged pain explodes
> to meet the clear blue of my tears
> sharp, razor,
> cutting pieces of my flesh
> your words,
> your hurts,
> you slash
> across my face
> across my back
> my tears join together, flowing
> ebbing towards my heart
> to wash away the debris
> to wash all poisons

from my gaping wounds
and yet
you stand before me
unashamed
you dare to look upon me
with no regard
for all you do
you walk upon me
as if I were your slave
to be owned and done with
as you please
It is with contempt
you glance,
and tread
and dance upon my breast
you tear,
you rip,
you shred
to leave a gaping wound
a gape for which there is no mend
that you can fix
I leave you now
I will not trouble you again
for I will be fine
without your greed,
your hatred,
your fear,
I need you no longer
I no longer care
for your abuse
I will be okay
when you are gone
Barbara-Helen Hill 1995

15

REALITY THERAPY

Reality Therapy is a counselling/therapy technique developed by Dr. William Glasser. He teaches that we all have basic needs: The need to survive and reproduce; the need to belong, to love, to share and cooperate; the need for power, not over others, but over self; the need for freedom; and the need for fun.

Love & Belonging - The need to belong, to have love and give love is as strong as the need to survive and instinctively procreate. Many adults remain in destructive relationships through repeated painful experiences such as beatings, arguments, threats, and sexual abuse because they fear they will have no love at all if they leave. Love at its worst is often seen as better than no love at all. Children abused by one parent often will defend that parent to the point of turning against the non-offending parent. It is especially true if the non-offending parent ignores the child or pays more attention to a sibling. Fear of abandonment can be a strong motivator especially if that abusive parent shows them love and attention in other ways. The script goes like this: "If I don't have close family friends and relatives, then life is hardly worth living." When talking to potential suicide victims, pay attention to their language. Nine times out of ten what they are really saying is that they don't feel like they belong.

In recovery we need a better kind of love. To get that kind of love we first need to give it to ourselves. We need to love and care about ourselves the way we want to be treated by others. The way to love ourselves is to meet our basic needs in ways that we ideally want to meet them and in ways that won't hurt us or others. Learning how to do this takes time, knowledge, and practice. I had to learn to give myself the love and attention that I wanted because I wasn't receiving it from outside. I didn't know what would make me happy until I began recovery and learned about the four basic needs that Dr. Glasser described. I learned that the work (overwork) that I was doing was meeting my needs for love and belonging as well as the need for power and fun. I felt a "part of" the group I worked with more so than with the family and friends. I had a history of hurts with my family – not that they intentionally hurt me, but I still felt the hurts. I trusted my co-workers more than my family at that time. Through recovery that has changed. My family, my friends, and my co-workers are all an important part of my life now.

Power & Control -Dr. Glasser describes the need for power as the drive to get others to obey us. Often the need for power in a person's life drives them to be active co-dependents. In actuality it is that little child inside that is feeling out of control. He does anything and everything to get his life back in order so that he can feel in control again. Often when we have a need for control, it comes out in a power struggle. Men, because of their physical strength, have historically come out with a greater share than women. Women, however, have no less a power need. This brings to mind another question about the lineage memory. If the lineage memory carries all our memories of past generations and is handed down much like the allergies and the addictions are said to be passed down, could it be that the lineage memory of women having equal power be coming out in the struggle for women's rights?

In the struggle for control, people believe that they can have control over another. That is not so. The only control a person can have is over him/herself. The people that use force and abuse to try to control only make life miserable for themselves and others. Even if they were to murder someone in their rage and struggle for power, do they really have control over the person?

The struggle for power gets confusing when it directly conflicts with the need for love and belonging. How can a person who has married for love and belonging feel that love when at the same time struggling to take over the marriage? The person tries harder and harder to make their partner "see it their way." The person ends up driving their partner away because of the inconsistent ways of behaving lovingly. What is tearing marriages apart is not lack of love but the need to control; the struggle for power. What tore my marriage apart, from my point of view, was not only the alcoholism but also the struggle between us – our struggle for power and love and belonging as Dr. Glasser states.

I wanted to have more of a say in my marriage. I didn't feel that I had a right and my husband continued to "be the boss" because I never spoke up for my rights. I didn't know I had rights. I fought for control and power by holding a full time job, going to college full-time, doing beadwork and sewing to make extra money. Besides all that I was trying to be a full-time mother as well. Our marriage fell apart. He drank; I became angry and worked harder and became the martyr. Unknowingly we both had control and power over our own lives but continued to blame each other.

There are satisfying ways of gaining power that are positive and do not keep others from meeting their needs. One way to meet your need for power is to receive recognition. This is available everyday at home, at school, or in the workplace. You can meet your need for power by being in charge – of projects, supervising people, or taking charge of yourself. You meet your need for power when you gain respect for yourself and others. You feel a sense of achievement when you accomplish a goal, and you gain another person's respect. Nothing can destroy a relationship as quickly as a lack of respect for the other person's thoughts or feelings. Each of us must have that need-fulfilling sense of importance, of believing that what we want is recognized.

Freedom - The need for freedom does not mean quitting the job, selling everything and buying a hippie van. It also doesn't mean getting a divorce and living in a harem, although a few years ago, people thought that's what it was. It means the freedom to make healthy

choices in your life such as how and where you live. You also need to have the freedom to choose what you want to read and write, and what, where, and how to pray if you choose to. If you don't have the freedom to make choices and gain some amount of control over your life, then you cannot meet your other basic needs. A difficulty arises when someone fighting for power needs tries to control, one who is fighting for their freedom needs. An example would be those who kill in wars. They say they are fighting for freedom. In actuality they are killing to have the freedom to tell other people what to do. One country is fighting for control over another and they, in turn, are fighting for their freedom. Thus the many wars that we have in the world.

Another conflict is the one between a need for freedom and the need for love and belonging. One partner wants the other to make a commitment to the relationship and the other partner wants to keep her/his options open. We are afraid to let our partner have her/his freedom because we might lose some of that love or what we feel is control. On the other hand, if we do try to control them, they may want their freedom badly enough to end the relationship. Those are tough choices in unhealthy relationships.

Communication can work wonders for married couples by talking to each other openly and honestly about what we want and don't want. As I stated before, I didn't trust in my life because of my history. I believe now that my husband didn't trust either. If he was drinking, then I would get angry and use the bill money to take the children to visit relatives or go on a shopping spree. My choices. I was acting out of anger not out of love for myself, my children, or my husband.

Learning to use freedom to make wise choices about the people, situations, and places in your life is worth all the time and effort it takes. Allow yourself the freedom to meet your needs. Allowing yourself to want what you want and go for it since you are not interfering with others who want to meet their needs. Learning about this in Reality Therapy has allowed me to make the choice in my life to remain alone. I have had the opportunity to heal the pain of past abuses and to grow into a healthier human being. Even if I have to experience loneliness at times.

When you limit yourself you are not meeting your need for freedom. But knowing what you have is often a lot less scary than not knowing what you might get. That is why many people stay in dead-end jobs or bad marriages. They are miserable, but at least they know what they have. Your need for freedom is deep. Your need for autonomy, for that ability to make choices in your life, is strong. When you do not make choices, or when you forget this need, then you do not feel happy with your life. To be happy with my life I need to feel that I have the right to make the choices that I do in my life and to experience the consequences of those choices – even if it is loneliness. Loneliness helps me to reach out to safe human beings and not to repeat the patterns of reaching for the bottle and abusive relationships.

Fun - "Fun is what you do when you don't have to do it." Mark Twain

The puritan influence on our culture has helped destroy the notion that having fun is acceptable behaviour. Our ancestors learned to enjoy human contact in many ways. Games, food, rituals, music, stories, and jokes helped our ancestors live together more harmoniously.

Children of trauma often ignore the need for fun. Anyone who has been the brunt of abuse or the eldest child who was responsible for siblings, often doesn't even know what fun is. We have to define fun. Dr. Glasser believes that fun is the basic genetic instruction for higher animals because that is the way they learn.

"The fact that learning is fun is a great incentive to assimilate what we need to satisfy our needs. Think back to a teacher whose lessons you vividly remember, and you will usually recall that whatever she taught, the class was fun. When we are both learning and having fun, we often look forward to hard work and long hours." (Control Theory, Glasser- pages 14,15)

Laughter is the best medicine. We often don't understand laughter or the reason we laugh. Dr. Glasser believes that for the moment, we experience a powerful sense that our need for fun is fulfilled. What is funny and causes us to laugh is that we are made aware of some new learning, some new awareness, or been shown some falseness to what we had believed for a long time. The pursuit of fun in our lives may take many turns. What was fun for you as a teenager may not be fun now. Or if you are in the process of finding your way in recovery, you may not know what fun is yet. To explore new things is fun. To try a new career or a hobby is fun.

In the earlier years of my recovery, I read everything that was printed about recovery. I continued to be in 12-step recovery and group counselling. I never took the time for fun because I didn't know what fun was in sobriety. My children were in Alateen for awhile, and we attended a few dry dances. It was all of a sudden fun to get up and dance, sober, and before eleven o'clock at night. I also found myself enjoying bowling with my kids. Even better, it was fun to go and sit by a lake or take a walk in the fields again. I especially enjoyed sitting on the floor with my niece and nephew reading.

I was free to go out and "just pretend we go bear hunting" in the woods next to my house, to read children's books, and finally, I found the opportunity to try my hand at painting again. Now I not only paint, write, and play music, I am even exploring singing and acting as well. I am learning to have fun in the arts, in nature, and finding that there are a lot of things that are fun and free.

Fun makes life brighter. Fun comes in many forms. Think of it as pleasure – it could be an evening walk with the dog, an all-night dance, or just paying the toll for the car behind you during rush hour as a surprise. Anything that can give you pleasure without hurting someone else.

The pursuit of fun may conflict with other needs in your life; for example, men watching sports on TV while the wife or children compete for attention. Some people become so obsessed for power that they have little room for fun.

In Reality Therapy we become aware of the fact that unhappiness in our lives comes from the picture in our minds of our wants, needs, and desires not matching what we have in reality. Rick Puteran, our Reality Therapy instructor, spoke to me personally of the four basic needs and pointed out how I had made choices to meet those needs. To meet the need for power and control, I had a job where I felt needed, wanted, loved, and supported. I was in control of my life, or so I thought. I had self power. But you will notice that I also mentioned that I felt needed, loved, and supported. I fulfilled both the need for power and the need for love and belonging in that job. Unfortunately, that left little time for my family. While meeting my needs, I may have denied the rest of my family the right to meet their own needs.

The dilemma is that we have a right to meet those needs in our own lives and so do the people we are responsible to as principle caregivers. If we pay attention to our own needs, each and every need, in a healthy way the world would be a much better place. We need to look at how we meet those needs – to make sure that the needs are really needs and not the inner child acting out in desperation.

The inner child needs to feel the love and belonging but it needs to feel it from you first. The inner child needs to feel in control because it lost control a long time ago. By setting boundaries and honouring those boundaries, you can help that child feel safe, loved, and in control. Then the child and you, as the adult, will feel more like having fun. If you are not paying attention to that inner child, if you don't support and honour the boundaries for your inner child, the child will act out. Relationship addiction? Sex addiction? Or even turning to the other addictions mentioned before such as turning to work, or gambling.

When the inner child begins to feel listened to and heard, she/he then starts to trust you and then will be more agreeable to meeting new people, trying new things, and having fun. When you feel at peace inside from the trust and love between you and your inner child, you feel more in control and the need to control others lessens. When you feel in control of your life you make wise choices, and there are no ill effects to suffer from those decisions. You are free to explore and enjoy life.

Reality Therapy gave me a focus. I knew about other needs in life like the need for shelter, food, water, clothes; all the basic needs for survival. But I wasn't aware of the other needs that Dr. Glasser pointed out. It made life so simple. Putting that with the 12-step programs, I was on my way to recovery. I had a long way to go but I now had a map. I wasn't stumbling in the dark.

In everything you do, you are either meeting your needs or not. In other words, if you don't make a decision you have made a decision. Nothing will change in your life if you don't do something different from what you have been doing.

Keep on doing what you are doing, and you keep on getting what you are getting.

16

THE PROCESS

Recovery takes on many faces just as abuse does. Recovery means taking responsibility for oneself, recognizing the pain, healing the wounds, and moving on responsibly. Emotional healing removes the pain of memories stored in the physical body and in the subconscious. It is the total healing of the physical, emotional, and mental bodies that leads to spiritual wellness. One needs to heal on all of the levels.

4 Levels of Healing - Healing takes place on four levels: emotional, spiritual, physical, and mental; and does not necessarily take place simultaneously. Each individual heals differently. Some people first need to become well physically or to "get fit." Others need to read self-help books and understand first. Other people need to go through a spiritual awakening through church, traditional ceremonies, 12-step meetings and/or meditation and guidance. Often it is a process of moving from one to the other. Sometimes a person needs to sober up at a 12-step meeting for a while and then, with spiritual guidance attend the church or ceremonies. Often because of abuses they do not return to either. They find their way with the 12-step program only.

Feelings/Emotions & Therapy - Emotions are energy in motion within our bodies. In the quiet space or in a counselling session, if one just breathes deeply and allows the feelings to come, and lets the tears flow; one will feel oneself at the top of an emotional hill, talking and remembering the trauma, and then go into a deeper feeling level. If allowed, one will feel those deep buried feelings. The person will find themselves at the top of the next emotional hill after she/he is done.

A person will not "get stuck" in that process. The spirit naturally pops back up spontaneously because one has released the burdening pain. Sometimes this process takes only minutes; sometimes it can take an hour or longer, depending on the therapist or helpers that one has and if the person can shut the brain down and stop it from being in control. Sometimes that is the hardest part. Allowing the brain to take a rest and let the feelings come in. If one has done this a few times and is used to this process, one can even do this alone. It is to provide the inner child with the safety they didn't feel as a child; it is to feel feelings.

Dissociation & Suppression of Feelings - We suppress our feelings during a traumatic experience due to fear, or lack of safety at the time. The suppressed spirit is hidden, traumatized, brutalized, and abused. A sexually abused or traumatized child feels abandoned by their caregivers, and will often abandon him/her self to protect themselves from feeling. They dissociate. Many people in therapy take a great deal of time just to get in touch with the self and to learn to trust him/her self again. The therapist or helper aids in the trust building.

One needs to take the time, through guided meditation or visualization to get in touch with that child. They need to start a little at a time to rebuild a foundation of trust. Full recovery requires allowing that child the feelings and validation that she/he did not feel as a child.

Naming Feelings -Feelings are deep and usually confusing. I like to name only five feelings. I find that when a person is deep in pain they very often cannot identify feelings by names. Using only five makes it easier for the person to identify and label feelings in their terms and to do the emotional healing around them. I think of them in layers: Anger, Fear, Hurt, Loneliness, Shame.

The recovery process is like peeling an onion. It is easier when dealing with a person who is constantly angry to say, what is under the anger? For example, I have found that the underlying feeling in men is fear. Society conditions men to believe that they do not feel fear. They are taught to be strong, aggressive, and whatever happens, not to have any emotions, especially fear. Women on the other hand, are told never to be angry, or to suppress it. Women were always to be loving, stoic, and forever soft.

Feelings are not bad; they are not wrong. One is not falling apart if she/he should feel. Sometimes one gets angry with him/her self when she/he gets scared and starts to cry. Many women start to cry when they get angry. Children learn from watching. How did you see your mother deal with anger? Did your mom withhold the anger and just seethe inside and then take out her anger on you? Did you see your dad rage after holding in his anger over many little things? Sometimes one may have received the brunt of the anger as dad beat him/her.

A person retains memories of what they learned or didn't learn about feelings and emotions and has to re-learn healthy ways to allow feelings in recovery. Often the names of the feelings are learned in baby steps. It is necessary to learn how they are felt in the body, and what to do.

Anger - It is okay to be angry but not okay to hurt oneself, or anyone else with anger. One of the most painful cases I had to hear, was the pain of a man whose family, his wife and children, were afraid of him. Inside was a little boy that was crying out for love and on the outside was a man that was oozing anger and rage. He did not know how to deal with those feelings and it resulted in him flying off the handle and being abusive.

It is okay and necessary to get anger out of your body and to let it go by giving voice to it. Sometimes one can get anger out of the body by doing constructive physical things. Kneading bread is a good way of expending energy. We can go outside and chop wood if there is that opportunity. A person also can beat your fists into the couch or bed. Lying on the floor and putting pillows under the feet to kick is good. We need to look for whatever way that will expel the energy without hurting oneself. Good long, brisk walks also help to expel the energy, especially if you are crying, yelling, or voicing your feelings in some way.

In getting rid of the anger, a person is usually in the little child stage. Allowing that child to release the anger in a non-abusive way gives him/her the opportunity to release the energy. Yelling, crying, voicing out loud, making growling noises from the belly, releases the energy.

Releasing painful emotions frees up clear thinking. A person cannot make good clear decisions while in emotional pain. Often when counselling a person, taking them on walks helps.

Fear - Allowing the release of fear can be frightening. The body can shake and tremble. It may require walking or running or physical action of some kind to release. Allowing the self to just shake is another way. A person needs to know it is okay to loosen the hands, and uncross the feet and legs, and allow him/her self to just shake. Allowing the trembling to continue until it stops of its own accord lessens the intensity.

I was to do a workshop with some women from my community when I met the lead counsellor, Donna Jenson, at the airport in Toronto. We went to the motel where she was to stay and we had a meeting with her, Bob Antone, and the other women of the team. We each had a counselling session with Donna and when it came to my turn, I couldn't get to my feelings. She had me start walking, pacing back and forth, and around in the room. Finally, after about ten minutes of walking and talking I could get to the fear.

I told Donna and the group of my fear because of what many people called my mixed blood and the things that I was hearing. Many people in my community had the anger towards the whites and the do-gooders, and they often voiced their anger about white people. I, of Mohawk and British ancestry, was taking in their anger and hadn't learned to let it go. I could cry and release that fear in the room with

Donna. She was able to help me see that I am okay just as I am and God doesn't see mixed bloods. God sees humans.

Hurt & Loneliness - Sometimes we confuse hurt with loneliness and the location where we perceive it in the body. Most often hurt is felt in the gut area, and loneliness around the heart area; however, each person is different. Most often, when the fear or the anger comes up, it is because it has been our mechanism used for coping when it wasn't safe to feel hurt or loneliness. Tears allow us to feel the hurt and the loneliness after finding out what lies under the fear and anger. Deep crying and sobbing comes in, releasing the immediate pain and releasing the pain from childhood.

Shame - Shame is often the hardest feeling to get to. One can carry the shame of her/his abusers. One can also carry the shame of the abused ancestors. Although the lineage memory carries shame and the other feelings, it also carries good teachings. The healing process allows a person to release shame and to find the good messages.

People release shame by deep sobbing and often by coughing and spitting. For women, in some cases, sexual abuse is released by the spontaneous return of menstrual flow or regulation of the flow. Each body is different and experiences body healing differently.

Shame is toxic. It causes us to abuse ourselves and others. Shame is often not ours to carry. A sexually abused child is not to blame. The adult person who abused the child is the one that should be carrying the shame. There is a difference between healthy guilt or conscience, and toxic shame. Conscience keeps one from doing things that are wrong. Shame makes one think that she/he is wrong.

Working with the body and the emotions simultaneously is an excellent method if one finds someone with that gift. We advise people in recovery to seek licensed massage therapists when the person feels safe enough. Some people have a hard time trusting to be able to allow someone to touch them. They must feel safe in order to process the feelings. One lady I know after going to her chiropractor to have adjustments made, experiences emotional healing within the next few hours or days. Another lady going to cognitive or psychological therapy, a few days later, after integrating the information, was able to release the emotional pain.

Toxic Feelings - One person was very angry when coming to see me. I would ask what is under the anger and they would get to the hurt immediately. They could differentiate between healthy anger and toxic, rageful anger. Un-released anger increases to become toxic. Layers build upon layers until it becomes toxic rage. Fear not acknowledged, validated, and released becomes debilitating and can result in phobias. Hurt and loneliness results in shutting down the heart. A person learns not to trust anyone and ends up not loving anyone fully. Recovering the self and healing emotional pains lead to love, love of self, and the Creator. It emanates out.

Memory & Body Pain - When one heals emotions, one frees up blocked space used by energy that is trying to keep those memories secret and stored safely out of the way. It takes more energy to suppress painful memories than it does to release the pain and let it go. With the release of the pain or grief we free the emotions to allow our mental capacity to expand.

It is said we use only ten percent of our brain capacity on a daily basis because of emotional blocks to learning. Each time there is a hurt or painful experience one stores it in the brain. We remember those things and can heal the emotional pain around those memories when the Creator feels we are ready.

Energy is continually used to suppress pain. One may use all forms of addictions and compulsions to suppress them. Many people have blocked all connections with their body memories because of abuses. When one is in the healing process, one needs to become connected with the body. It is most important when dealing with sexual and physical abuse.

Physical Healing -The physical body stores most of the abuse memories. In the recovery process a good therapist will continually ask you where the feeling is in the body and to get in touch with your body. Our feelings must be in sync with what we are thinking.

Physical healing takes many forms. I have a favorite book that I keep with me, <u>You Can Heal Your Body</u>, by Louise Hay. Whenever a person asks me or complains about a physical ailment, I refer them to the book and we look up the ailment. It is amazing how the physical ailment is usually right on, in relation to where they were emotionally. It is a good guide to help them heal whatever memory is coming up for them.

I encourage a person to get a good physical examination with a reliable doctor. I also encourage people to seek doctors with a healthy attitude. As a recovering alcoholic or drug addict, a person must be able to tell the doctor that they have addictions and need help to deal with any ailments without narcotics, if possible. There are doctors out there who only promote prescription use and abuse but there are also doctors out there who are also recovering. We need to value ourselves enough to seek a healthy doctor.

Basic & Spiritual Needs - Learning about our needs, both basic and spiritual needs, is the first step. We need to know our rights as a human being coming into this world. We need to know what our unmet needs were and that we can now as adults, re-parent and provide our inner child with those needs.

We need to be seen and heard when we communicate. We grew up with the old adage that, children were to be seen and not heard. I was often told to go outside and play because I was to be seen and not heard. I took that message literally and became a person that even tried to disappear. I would find places to hide. I would go and sit in a tree, and often talk to the trees, the spirits, the little people, trying to be heard. Recovery allowed me to heal the pain and to accept the fact that I may not always be listened to. It took a long time for me to experience the feeling of being heard. We need to be honest with ourselves to experience being honest with others. If one is talking recovery and spouting all the words while still behaving abusively, then one will not have the feeling of being accepted and believed.

One needs to know that others have faith and trust in us, but one needs to feel that trust within the self first. Often one goes through life working and striving to the point of exhaustion, trying to prove to someone else that she/he has a right to be there.

Boundary Setting & The Need for Security - To feel secure about and at peace with oneself comes with boundary setting. It comes with trust building and honouring the requests of the inner child. Experiencing an uncomfortable feeling near another person may mean a re-stimulation of some trauma experienced in the past. Healing work will remove the pain and that person will no longer stimulate that pain.

Healing the pain does not re-traumatize the inner child. It helps the inner child to recognize that this person is not the abuser from the past. It also sets up the trust that one is listening to the inner child and that can become her/his barometer for setting boundaries. If that inner child still does not feel comfortable around that person then one can keep her/his distance. To not engage in anything that is going to make her/him feel uncomfortable or unsafe is to set boundaries. You have a right to say no. You have a right to remove yourself from situations where you feel uncomfortable.

Abandonment - Another need is to feel that one's existence is not detrimental but beneficial to the important people in one's life. Meeting these needs takes time because as children these needs were not met. Often we were given chores and jobs that were beyond our capabilities. We felt like failures and often were treated as "dumb" and "stupid." These words from parents and caregivers are devastating because we are being condemned by the very people who have given us life; the very ones who are supposed to love us and keep us safe; the ones who were supposed to be there to nurture and teach us with love.

I heard that one could not be abandoned when they could take care of themselves, say after the age of seven or eight. I tend to doubt that. I maintain that one can feel abandonment at any age. As an adult, a person who was mistreated as a child and carries abandonment issues will have tremendous trouble with relationships. I have even felt the spiritual abandonment of being born. During a counselling session I was able to feel the pain of leaving the Creator and having to be born, and of having the feeling of not being wanted. Abandonment is the feeling that entraps most of us. Fear of abandonment often directs our daily living. We work really hard to be accepted, at work, at school, at home, and even with ourselves.

Mistreatment will inevitably cause the child to retreat within. The inner child will disappear and the false self will emerge. For those who don't understand "the Inner Child concept" think of the character defects as mentioned in the 12-Step recovery program.

Mistreatment causes the loss of the inner child and that loss results in the ultimate abandonment. People, abandoned emotionally, physically, and/or spiritually find that abandonment is the most traumatic experience to work through.

The Inner Child & Sexuality - Feelings between two people can become confused, especially in a marriage. Partners can re-stimulate old memories, and pain, unintentionally by being themselves. When this happens, the inner child needs validation. When the child has its needs met in a healthy way, then the adult can meet her/his adult partner in a healthy adult relationship. If the inner child is "out there" due to re-stimulation of a traumatic experience, then that child will experience abuse of many kinds, including sexual abuse or what will seem like sexual abuse.

Inner child healing takes place on a daily basis. The spontaneous, fun loving, creative, child is not lost anymore. With continuous support and nurturing, the inner child is freed to be more of the spontaneous, fun loving, creative person it was naturally meant to be.

Reclaiming Power - The process of recovery includes action, plus awareness, plus contact with others of like mind. All of these components equal reclamation of power. A person becomes aware, and contacts others who are also becoming aware. We seek help and put into action what we think about for recovery. We cannot just sit back and dream of a healthier life. We must go after it with action. One begins to reclaim power and so reclaim the self.

We can choose to stay a victim or get out of it. If a person can identify their "Ethnostress" pattern, and define the lifelines or family patterns, it can help them to trust. We trust, that persons we need will be put in our path. A person can ask him/her self: What ways have I been keeping myself victimized? What do I need to do to improve or change my life? Understand re-stimulation teaching, and clear thinking counselling. Learn about boundaries and co-dependency and have faith.

Openness to Healing Guidance - When one is beginning recovery one needs to sober up or stop the compulsions and addictions. The first step is the willingness to be open to hearing the messages that the Creator is sending. It could be a phrase someone says or by reading something in a book. Or it could be the death of someone, as in my case. I lost my dad on August 13, 1981to an alcohol related disease. A month later, on September 9, I lost my husband to the same disease–alcohol. My dad died of liver complications. My husband died of a heart attack after going into DT's or Delirium Tremens – he was only 38. That was my impetus for seeking help.

Dreams & Recovery - Recovery does not just take place in the therapist's office dealing with psychology. Healing takes place on a daily basis, at work, school, home, driving the car, walking etc. It takes place quite often in the dreams as well, in confronting fears in dreams to overcome them. For example, I have faced my fear of snakes in my sleep. I can now recognize them as part of "all my relations." Dreams have allowed me to face fears which I have had in my sexual abuse recovery. I was lying on my bed in my apartment, sleeping and coming out of sleep. I got to the semi-dream state and could see a dark brown hand reaching for me under the covers. Simultaneously I saw this young girl, or felt this young girl walk across my bed and leave the room.

When I awoke I wrote everything down in my journal and felt the confusion and fear, "Was it real; were they ghosts; or what the heck was it?" I called my friend and asked for feedback. I was assured that I was okay, and that I wasn't crazy. Maybe it was time to start looking at the sexual abuse recovery. With my counselling help I was able to see the abuse, heal the pain around it and to help the young girl see that it wasn't her fault. She didn't cause it and she doesn't need to run away anymore. I had been running away from the recovery of my sexual abuse by getting into the food addiction.

Meditation & Recovery -I have found that the joy comes from the willingness to let go, and to let the Creator guide us — to look within to do what one enjoys. I have found that to be free to heal oneself, to be at one with all of Creation is to allow one's self to sit quietly and meditate and to listen for the guidance. We can do this ourselves without help.

We need to be careful not to discount our self when looking outside to Native elders and Christian religious leaders for help. Not all priests or elders are healthy themselves. One does not get to be an elder just because one reaches the age of fifty. One has to earn that through one's own learning, experience, and healing, particularly self healing of past traumas and hurts. Just because a person is a priest, or minister, or elder, does not make them wiser. We should not discount the power within ourselves. We do not need an interpreter between ourselves and the Creator. Talking to the Creator is no different from talking to one's partner, child, or even oneself. One just needs to say what is in her/his heart and then take time to listen.

Hearing from the Creator is just as easy as listening. With no TV, radio, books, or people, to distract in a quiet room or outside in nature, we can listen to the stillness. Listening to the small voice, letting the subconscious thoughts come through. One needs to ask the smart, intellectual self to take a vacation. It will not die. One needs opportunity to take some time to talk with the Creator. Then invite the smart intellectual self back. The brain can use the rest. It has worked hard to keep the body alive and well through many traumas.

I have experienced deep feelings while in the quiet space with the self and the Creator. Memories come, and with those memories, tears. That's okay. We release the tears to heal the pain.

Recovery means taking one step at a time. In recovery, a person needs to have support, as a group or individual that will validate him/her on every level. Validation is for the adult and the inner child. It's necessary to enable the child to grow, to have the opportunity for the four parts of us to integrate so that the person in healing can become a strong, loving, spiritual being, the kind we were all meant to be.

17

FINAL FEW WORDS

What I've learned since the first edition in 1996 is that the healing trauma and abuse will take place if you are willing to work and care for yourself. Your counsellor, therapist, support person cannot do it for you. They are there to guide you.

The gift of healing has been given to me by the Creator and I share that gift with anyone who will listen. There are also the gifts of kindness, honesty, love, and faith. They have been given to me and I share them because without sharing I will lose whatever I have been given. An elder once said that he must share his teachings in order to keep them. In other words, if we are stingy with our gifts they can be taken away.

My daughter said that I taught her that you are never recovered, you are recovering every day. So she thought I should continue to write every day, and when my last day is here on earth, she will write my last chapter. I thought that was a good tribute to the teachings of the Creator. Through the 12-steps and traditions, the traditional Native teachings, and the teachings of the Creator; everything that I have learned I shared with them. In addition to that I've encouraged them to seek their own path. We've all experienced not only the Longhouse ceremonies of the Haudenosaunee – our home, but we've been invited and attended Ojibway Ceremonies with one of my friends in central Ontario and of course we've attended church with my mom. There have been many sources of teachings for faith, honesty, sharing, and kindness.

Seeking spirituality in many forms comes with growth and that comes with emotional healing.

In 1988 my son Tim thanked me for allowing him to watch me grow up, and now my daughter Monica was offering me the opportunity for my book to continue, with her writing the final chapter.

While writing this book in Western Canada, I kept thinking about the Haudenosaunee people, my people and the teachings that come from our history. The White Roots of Peace go out in four directions and our teachings tell us that anyone that wishes may come to the source and find healing, peace, and truth as long as he believes in the Creator and follows the Great Law in his heart. My friends the Ojibway, Cree, Sioux and Blackfoot have told me about the medicine wheel, the sweat lodge and four directions.

I couldn't find a title and I asked my friend Beth to read a draft of the manuscript and see if she could pick a title. She said the title jumped right out when she read the poem, Maggie. That poem was written for a dear sweet lady who taught me a lot during her time here on earth. I was and I still feel part of her family, and was shown unconditional love by her daughter Rosie and her family. They are very important to me and I have great memories of them and the Longhouse and the times that we sang and danced to the rattles. I see the healing taking place in myself and others like the shaking of the rattles.

The rattles start out in one form and through the craftsmanship of a person they end up in another form. I started out in one way, addicted, compulsive, co-dependent, and with the help of people who are gifted in their craft of healing I have found myself to be in recovery. Every day, I see myself being shaken and reminded that the Creator is here, ready to help me to remove another piece of the trauma of colonization. Today the work is done with my writing.

In 1997, my son Mike and I reunited and he brought me the gift of a grand-daughter. Now we have a real family; my two sons and their wives, a daughter and her husband. There are four grand-daughters, including one "borrowed," (my son's step-daughter) and two grand-sons including one "borrowed" (my daughter's step-son) As of this writing in 2017, my grand-daughter is pregnant with my third great-grand-son. I am blessed beyond measure.

APPENDICES: PHYSIOLOGY OF ADDICTIONS

Alcohol - Alcohol has been one of the deadliest killers of Indigenous people since smallpox. In historical times the colonizers, specifically the traders, laced alcohol with laudanum and other chemicals to make the substance deadlier. They knew that a drunk would trade for less than the value of the furs and would probably trade for more alcohol.

Many people around the world are recovering alcoholics and many are still suffering. Indigenous people who once had respect for everything have also become addicted, and have lost respect for many things, especially themselves.

I was asked to do a presentation on the effects of alcohol on the body and nutrition. I got this book <u>Nutrition - Concepts and Controversies</u> by Eva May Hamilton and Eleanor Whitney. It is a text from a University Program and has wonderful information – too much for the presentation and this book. Their words are italicized.

> *Alcohol is a tranquilizer, sedative, and general all-around anti-depressant. It is also the most abused legal drug available and the drug likely to cause us the greatest amount of permanent physiological damage, not to mention the mind-altering behaviours that we may loosely label as "drunkenness."*

Contrary to popular belief, it is a depressant, not a stimulant. It is an anesthetic just like ether. The first effect on the brain is to slow down the area that controls judgment and thought.

Alcohol is especially damaging to the liver, the stomach, small intestines, pancreas, adrenal glands, brain, and nerve pathways. These organs play vital roles in processing and storing the nutrients obtained from food. Introduce alcohol, and all else must be put aside so that the body can begin dealing with this enemy that has invaded the system. Changing the toxic alcohol into a non-toxic form takes priority over every other digestive process.

When alcohol is present, vitamins and minerals are poorly absorbed and under used. An alcoholic is likely to be poorly nourished even if his or her diet contains every essential and nonessential nutrient known.

Alcohol irritates mucous membranes; especially the esophagus, stomach, and small intestines. Alcohol is the number one junk food. It provides nothing in the way of nutrients; it only provides unneeded and unwanted calories.

Alcohol interferes with the production of the neurotransmitters in the brain, and people begin to transpose thoughts, phrases, words, places, dates, and facts into drunken babbling.

We assume you are not willing to die before your time. So you are left with the challenge of rebuilding, nourishing, and strengthening the precious gift of life that is yours.
Some allergy specialists believe that somewhere in the family tree of every highly allergic person is at least one alcoholic.

That is what I meant by Lineage Memory. If you have no awareness of an alcoholic in your immediate family, a little tracing may find that somewhere out there on a limb of that family tree is a great-uncle" something or other" who was an alcoholic. If your body craves certain foods, you become allergic to them and crave them even more, just like that alcoholic.

Fetal Alcohol Syndrome and Fetal Alcohol Effects are more prominent in today's society than ever before, some to a greater degree than others. Many communities are actively campaigning against drinking, especially while pregnant.

Adult Children of Alcoholics is an organization that started because of the effects of alcohol on children. Alcohol affects all parts of the body and the relationships. When you think about the alcoholics in the world remember the pain they are going through. Is part of the pain a result of Lineage Memory? Is alcoholism a disease that is hereditary? Is it a symptom of the underlying problems such as colonialism and oppression?

Alcohol prior to the coming of the Europeans, was for ceremonial use and was from the natural fermentation of foods. It wasn't chemically induced. More information for your consideration:

Changing One Addiction for Another - *There are other substances we might choose (unconsciously or consciously) to replace the alcohol when we decide to give up that drink. Alcoholics have a very neat system that allows them to trade their addiction to alcohol for another addiction. Once an addictive lifestyle is in place, changing to another way of thinking and behaving is extremely difficult. When the alcohol is out of your system, the patterns of behaviour that made your addiction to it possible continue to function in your life. It is easy to replace the alcohol with candy (sugar), cigarettes, coffee, gambling, work, sex, relationships, and of course drugs.*

Eating disorders are most likely to replace alcohol addiction and to perpetuate the behavioral pattern that got you addicted in the first place. Both offer immediate gratification. You begin to eat the way you were drinking - to excess and, with little or no regard for the consequences.

The people around you are so delighted with your having given up alcohol that they generally ignore the fact that you have traded one addiction for another. We are often guilty of encouraging the overeating, particularly in the early stages of treatment and recovery.

Almost any food can become addictive. A person who feels he or she must have a certain type of food daily, who experiences withdrawal symptoms when it is not available, has a food addiction. For some, this is a psychological reaction to a food that gives comfort in a time of stress.

One friend of mine in British Columbia stated that she probably could become addicted to celery because of her history.

Caffeine - Somewhere in your mind was lurking the fact that alcohol as well as caffeine and nicotine are all bad for you. With any one of them there is the possibility of developing nutritional deficiencies or perhaps imbalances that can lead to physical symptoms.

Ulcers are a clear and present danger from the abuse of all three of these substances. The blood sugar suffers also. The blood sugar levels get on a sort of roller coaster when any one substance is used, but the use of more than one heightens the effect.

Caffeine and related substances act as stimulants to both the central nervous system and the heart. Caffeine also stimulates gastric secretions, acts as a smooth-muscle relaxant, and increases the need to urinate. It causes enough stress like reactions in the body to raise the blood sugar (glucose) and free up fatty acids, which also circulate in the blood. Starting down in your stomach, caffeine causes increased secretion of acid, which in turn might be enough to cause an ulcer. Some medical researchers have reported that instant and decaffeinated coffee are even more potent stimulants of acid than regular coffee or even pure caffeine.

Nicotine - Tobacco was given to the people of North America as a medicine, and it was used ceremonially.

Europeans, after being introduced to it, made a substantial living from this plant. *Cigarettes, cigars, snuff or smokeless tobacco, have been blamed for countless numbers of deaths relating to heart attacks, cancer, and other health problems. Nicotine interferes with the absorption of calcium and is often a primary factor in the development of adult bone loss, called osteoporosis. Nicotine interferes with the absorption of other minerals, causing imbalances that could eventually produce deficiency syndromes in persons with poor nutrition. Smoke and nicotine irritate the mucous membranes of both the lungs and the gastrointestinal tract. This irritation of the lining of the stomach increases the risk of ulcers.*

Stress accompanies the use of nicotine because a stress like reaction occurs when the nicotine stimulates the adrenal glands in your body thus raising blood sugar levels. One cigarette suppresses your appetite for 15 to 60 minutes, so smokers frequently smoke instead of eating, or they delay their intake of food. The suppression of appetite occurs because of three factors; increase of blood sugar levels, deadening of taste buds and the inhibiting of stomach contractions. The use of nicotine also increases the metabolic rate, so smokers eat more and gain less weight.

When people mention that they want to quit smoking and don't know how, I advise them to think of how tobacco was used by their ancestors looking back many generations. When you go to light up a cigarette, remember that they used tobacco for prayer in their pipes. What you think while you smoke may be construed as prayer. What are you thinking as you smoke? What are you praying for? Tobacco wasn't given to us for abuse, it was given to us for use, and like everything else the Creator made, it is to be taken care of and replenished in a good way.

Sugar - Sugar was not a natural part of the North American diet. It was introduced like many other substances, by the colonizers. Sugar is one of the main problems for those people with eating disorders, especially those that come from alcoholic backgrounds and or alcoholic families.

Many Indigenous people suffer from diabetes in North America, and that is due to diet. Intake of sugar and or other foods that we are not hereditarily used to is causing more deaths among our people.

Some experts believe that sugar affects the mental functions as well as the mood of an individual. Like any drug, sugar can be addicting. The determination is whether we use the substance – sugar, vitamins, or drugs – for altering mood or body sensations. If a person cannot go for a time without using the substance, then it may be an addiction.

Sugar is not a poison; it is a source of carbohydrate calories. It contributes no vitamins, minerals, fiber, protein, or other substance of redeeming value to the body's nutritional requirements. The average fast-food hamburger contains approximately nine

teaspoons of sugar. Recovering persons use sugar to help them get through the difficult period of withdrawal from alcohol and to deal with fluctuations in their blood-sugar level. This is part of the recovery process.

Used in abundance as a mood-altering substance, sugar becomes addicting. Sugar is a depressant and consumed in large amounts it affects the opiate receptor sites in the central nervous system. As the sedative or relaxing effects of sugar wear off, you experience agitation or a feeling of being "hyper." This rebound reaction that starts that old roller coaster feeling of first up and then down just like the cross-use between alcohol, caffeine, and nicotine. Sugar, when combined with caffeine, has even a more addicting effect. Using large amounts of coffee loaded with sugar is essentially the same as combining an upper and a downer. Again the use of soda pop and chocolate as a "soother," is of particular problem with people with eating disorders.

Sugar substitutes have the sweetness of sugar without the calories but the non-nutritive sweetener only tastes sweet and does not satisfy appetite. This accounts for the fact that some persons consume more high-fat foods when they use sugar substitutes. They do this convinced that having "saved calories" with the non-nutritive sweetener, they can make up the difference elsewhere. But some non-nutritive sweeteners increase the appetite and add to the problem rather than reduce it. Aspartame has been proven to increase feelings of hunger and decrease feelings of fullness within an hour of eating foods that contain it. The theory has been advanced that aspartame may disrupt the appetite control centre of the brain and cause the person using it to eat more rather than less.

Learn to prefer foods with very little or no sweetener of any kind added. Learn to really enjoy the taste, aroma, and full bodied flavor that nature provides us in so many fruits and vegetables. You will be better off nutritionally and spiritually.

If you feel you have been overusing sugar and sugar substitutes consider the possibility that you may be trading one addiction — alcohol, for another– sugar. Isn't dealing with one addiction just about enough? Life can be sweet for you on a natural basis.

There are many foods out there that contain sugar: stuffing and bread mixes, canned and dried soups, peanut butter, frozen pizza, soy sauce, gravy mixes, dips for chips, salad dressings, meat tenderizers, spices, frozen and canned vegetables, frozen dinners, bouillon cubes, garlic salt, cereals, crackers, and table salt. When you eat eight ounces of flavored yogurt you get six teaspoons of sugar. One ounce of cold cereal contains two to five teaspoons of sugar and your favorite soda of twelve ounces contains ten to twelve teaspoons of sugar depending on the type.

Remember Coca Cola at one time contained cocaine. It now contains massive amounts of caffeine and sugar. I am told that they lace cigarette papers with opium and cure the tobacco with sugar. Ever wonder why it is so hard to give up smoking and why some people become addicted to Coke and Pepsi? Maybe the sugar and the other additives have something to do with it.

Nutrition: Concepts and Controversies

by Eva May Hamilton and Eleanor Whitney West Publishing Company
50 West Kellogg Boulevard
P.O. Box 3526
St. Paul, Minnesota 55165 1979

RIGHTS

All women have a right to positive, healthy sexuality. Incest survivors, having this right, can redefine sexuality for themselves and develop ways of relating sexually with others who feel good to them. To ensure against further abuse and to create healthy, positive sexual experiences, survivors must make sure certain basic conditions are met. Though these conditions may vary somewhat from person to person, the five that follow (called CERTS) seem essential:

CERTS for Positive, Healthy Sexuality

Consent: I can freely and comfortably choose whether or not to engage in sexual activity. I am able to stop the activity at any time during sexual contact.

Equality: My feeling of personal power is on an equal level with my partner. Neither of us dominates the other.

Respect: I have a positive regard for myself and for my partner. I feel respected by my partner. I feel supportive of my partner and supported by my partner.

Trust: I trust my partner on both a physical and emotional level. We have a mutual acceptance of vulnerability and an ability to respond to it with sensitivity.

Safety: I feel secure and safe within the sexual setting. I am comfortable with and assertive about where, when and how the sexual activity takes place. I feel safe from the possibility of unwanted pregnancy and/or sexually transmitted diseases.

When these conditions are met, sexual activity can become fun, nurturing, and a true expression of caring. It's a natural human response to want to be physically close to people who one cares for, to share love and appreciation with a hug, handshake or kiss. With an intimate partner, under circumstances of mutual respect and consent, this caring can be expressed further with touch involving sensitive, private parts of the body. Each person sharing sexually can feel in control. The couple focuses on feeling emotionally at ease and close, not on one person getting something from the other. Defining sexual expression in the context of nurturing, healing closeness can help survivors to consider claiming sexuality as something beneficial for themselves. Experiencing sex when the body, mind, and emotions are united in pleasurable desire is something totally different from being sexually abused, and definitely worth the effort it takes to overcome the sexual traumas of the abuse.

(Malts & Holman 1987:9)

14 CORE ISSUES IN THE RECOVERY OF OUR CHILD WITHIN

Taken from the publication, <u>Healing the Child Within</u> by Charles Whitfield

Control
e.g. No matter what we think we have to control, whether someone else's behaviour, our own or someone else. We cannot control life, so the more that we try to control it, the more out of control we feel because we are focusing so much attention on it. Frequently the person who feels out of control is obsessed with the need to be in control.

Trust
e.g. Being supportive requires loyalty and trust from both the giver and the receiver. A person cannot betray another person's True Self for long without causing serious damage to the relationship. In order to grow, the Child Within should feel trusted and be able to trust others.

Feelings
e.g. Our feelings are how we perceive ourselves. They are our reaction to the world around us. Without awareness of our feelings, we have no real awareness of life. They summarize our experience and tell us if it feels good or bad. There are two basic kinds of feelings joyful and

painful. Joyful feelings make us feel a sense of strength, well being and completion. Painful feelings interfere with our sense of well being, use up our energy and can leave us feeling drained, empty and alone. They are telling us something, a message to our self that something important may be happening, something that may need our attention.

Being Over-Responsible

e.g. Many have learned to become overly responsible. That often seemed the only way to avoid many of our feelings, such as anger, fear, hurt. It also gave us the illusion of being in control. Instead of being over-responsible, other people may be irresponsible, passive and feel as if they are the victims of the world.

Neglecting Our Own Needs

e.g. Disowning and neglecting our own needs is intimately related to being over-responsible. It is connected to the hierarchy of basic human needs.

All-Or-None Thinking and Behaving

e.g. Either we love someone completely or we hate them. There is no middle ground. We see people around us as either good or bad, and not the composite they really are. We judge ourselves equally harshly. We may become attracted to others who think and behave in an all-or-none fashion.

High Tolerance for Inappropriate Behaviour

e.g. We grow up not knowing what is normal, healthy or appropriate. Having no other reference point on which to test reality, we think our family and their life, with its inconsistency, its trauma and its suffering, is "the way it is." We assume the role of our false or co-dependent self and we don't realize that there is any other way to be.

Low Self-Esteem (Shame)

e.g. It is the uncomfortable or painful feeling that we experience when we realize that a part of us is defective, bad, incomplete, rotten, phony, inadequate or a failure. We feel shame for being something wrong or bad. Our false self pretends not to have the shame, and would never tell anyone about it. Shame makes us believe that others can see through us, or our facade, into our defectiveness. We feel hopeless, isolated and lonely with our shame, as though we were the only one who has the feeling. We may say, "I'm afraid to tell you about it because if I do, you'll think I'm bad, and I can't stand hearing how bad I am," or "I may disguise my shame as if it were some other feeling or action and then project that onto other people."

Being Real
e.g. Our false self is a cover-up. It is inhibited, contracting and fearful. It is our egocentric ego and super-ego. Our false self is other-oriented, focusing on what it thinks others want it to be; it is over-conforming. It covers up, hides or denies feelings. It is often inappropriately aggressive and/or passive. It tends to be the "critical parent." It avoids playing and having fun. It pretends to be "strong" and even "powerful." Because it needs to withdraw and be in control, it sacrifices nurturing or being nurtured. It is self-righteous and attempts to block information coming from the subconscious. Most of the time in this role we feel uncomfortable, numb, empty, or in a false state. We sense that something is wrong and is missing. We often feel like this false self is the way we "should be." It is our public self who we think others and eventually even we think we should be.

Grieving our Un-Grieved Losses
e.g. Unresolved grief festers like a deep wound covered by scar tissue, a pocket of vulnerability ever ready to break out anew. When we experience a loss or trauma it stirs up everything within us that needs to be discharged. When we do not, the stress builds up to a state of chronic distress. This is stored within us as discomfort or tension that may at first be difficult to recognize. We may feel it or experience it through a wide range of manifestations, such as chronic anxiety, tension, fear or nervousness, anger or resentment, sadness, emptiness,

un-fulfillment, confusion, guilt, shame, or "no feelings at all." These destructive behaviours may cause us and others unhappiness, get us into trouble and can cause crisis after crisis. Message: "don't feel or don't talk about it."

Fear of Abandonment.
e.g. This goes all the way back to our earliest seconds, minutes, and hours of existence. Related to the issue of trust and distrust, it is often exaggerated among children who grew up in troubled or dysfunctional families. To counter this fear, we often mistrust; we shut out our feelings so we don't feel the hurt. Some is from their parents threatening to leave or abandon them as a disciplinary measure when they were infants and young children. This cruelty and trauma that may appear benign to some on the surface.

Difficulty Resolving Conflict.
e.g. This is a core recovery issue for adult children. It touches and interacts with most of the other core issues. We learn to avoid conflict whenever possible. When conflict occurs, we learn mostly to withdraw from it in some way. Occasionally, we become aggressive and try to overpower those with whom we are in conflict. When these techniques fail, we may become devious and attempt to manipulate. "I can do it on my own."

13 & 14. Difficulty Receiving and Giving Love
e.g. We believe we are not worthy of receiving love. Rather than believe we are unloved we can shift to believing that we do not need love. "I don't want to be loved," and then to "I will reject love no matter who gives it to me." We end up with "frozen feelings" or an inability to fully experience feelings and emotions including love.

Recovery is often where we experience unconditional love and begin to feel the healing effects of love. With love (nurturing) the nurturing person must be able to nurture and the person in need must be able to let go in order to be nurtured. It takes several years of being loved to get well and stay well. And then we can begin to love others in return. We no longer have to be afraid of love or to run away from it because we know that it is inside us as the core and healing part of our inner child.

POSITIVE CHARACTERISTICS

I am learning it's okay to be different from other people and that being "normal" is no longer important to me.

I am gaining the courage to face my problems.

I am learning to follow through and complete projects, set attainable goals, organize and pace myself.

I am learning that I have options that will allow me to make decisions.

I am learning to be truthful with myself and authentic with others, that telling the truth won't hurt me and to say "I made a mistake" and mistakes mean growth.

I am learning not to dwell on negatives or transfer my negatives to others.

I am learning to live and let live.

I am learning to have more confidence and believe in myself as well as accepting myself as I am, not an under-or over-achiever.

I am learning to let things go and turn things over to my Higher Power.

I am learning to appreciate the little things in life and enjoy life as it is, whatever the circumstances. I can have fun by assuming the responsibility for my fun.

I am learning not to take myself so seriously.

I am learning to be more open and adaptable and not push people away, to be more trustful in intimate relationships, to avoid destructive relationships, and to walk away from existing relationships that are unhealthy.

I am learning to live life for myself and not for the approval of others.

I am learning not to control or "save" others.

I am learning to understand me by listening to my inner feelings and avoid compulsive behaviour that seeks immediate gratification.

I am learning to stand up for myself and cope with problems not related to alcohol.

I am learning to be loyal, when not to be loyal and most of all, to be loyal to myself.

I am learning to be significant to the Creator.

I am learning that everything that I need, I have at this moment.

I AM THE BEST I CAN BE RIGHT NOW.

Note:

This information was taken from a handout with no particular identification of whom the author was. I by no means intended to plagiarize and apologize if offense is taken.

RULES FOR BEING HUMAN

You will receive a body. You may like it or hate it, but it will be yours for the entire period this time around.

You will learn lessons. You are enrolled in a full-time informal school called LIFE. Each day in this school you will have the opportunity to learn lessons. You may like the lessons or think them irrelevant or stupid. It makes no difference; you will learn lessons.

There are no mistakes, only lessons. Growth is a process of trial and error, experimentation. The "FAILED" experiments are as much a part of the process as the experiment that ultimately "WORKS."

A lesson is repeated until learned. A lesson will be presented to you in various forms until you have learned it. When you have learned it, you can then go on to the next lesson.

Learning lessons does not end. There is no part of life that does not contain its lessons. If you are alive, there are lessons to be learned.

"THERE" is no better than "HERE." When your "THERE" has become "HERE" you will simply obtain another "THERE" that will again, look better than "HERE."

Others are merely mirrors of YOU. YOU cannot love or hate something about another person unless it reflects to YOU something you love or hate about yourself.

What you make of life is up to YOU. YOU have all the tools and resources that YOU need. What YOU do with them is up to YOU. The choice is YOURS.

The answers to life's questions lie inside YOU. All YOU need to do is look, listen, and trust.

You will get what YOU ask for. It may not be what you wanted, but it will be what you asked for.

Anonymous

NATIVE VALUES

I received a handout at a Native Women's conference in Phoenix Arizona. There was no author's name or credit given but I'm including it in this book because I think it is a valuable piece of information.

Vision, or wholeness, is the spiritual core surrounded by Respect.

Respect is an honouring of the unified inner-connectedness of all of life which is a relationship that is mutual and interpersonal. The main Native values inspired from this core Vision and viewpoint of **Respect is explained as:**

KINDNESS: Capacity for caring and desire for harmony and well-being in interpersonal relations.

HONESTY: To act with the utmost honesty and integrity in all relationships recognizing the natural independence that is not to be dishonored, dignity, and freedom of oneself and others.

SHARING: Recognizing interdependence and interrelatedness of all of life, to relate with one another with an ethic of sharing, generosity, and collective/communal consciousness and cooperation.

STRENGTH: Conscious of the need for kindness and respecting the integrity of oneself and others, to exercise strength of character, fortitude and self-mastery in order to generate and maintain peace, harmony, and well-being within oneself and the total collective community.

BRAVERY: The exercise of courage and bravery on the part of the individual so that the quality of life and natural independence of oneself and others can be exercised in an atmosphere of security, peace, dignity, and freedom.

WISDOM: The respect for that quality of knowing and gift of vision in others (striving for the same within oneself) that encompasses the holistic view, possesses spiritual quality, and is expressed in the experiential breadth and depth of life. A person who embodies these qualities and actualizes it in others and translates it for others' benefit deserves respect as an "elder."

HUMILITY: The recognition of yourself as a sacred and equal part of the creation and the honouring of all life which is endowed with the same natural freedom, dignity, and equality. This leads to sensitivity towards others, a posture of non-interference, and a desire for good relations and balance with all life.

BIBLIOGRAPHY
(IN NO PARTICULAR ORDER)

CONTROL THEORY
A New Explanation of How We Control Our Lives
by William Glasser, M.D.
Harper & Row, Publishers, Inc., 10 East 53 Street,
New York, N.Y. USA 10022 or in Canada
Fitzhenry & Whiteside Limited, Toronto

BASIC CALL TO CONSCIOUSNESS
Akwasasne Notes
Akwasasne Mohawk Territory
P.O. Box 366,
Rooseveltown, N.Y. USA 13683

THE THIRST FOR WHOLENESS
Attachment, Addiction, and the Spiritual Path
by Christina Grof
HarperCollins Publishers, 10 East 53rd Street,
New York, N.Y. USA 10022

INCEST and SEXUALITY
A Guide to Understanding and Healing
by Wendy Maltz,
Beverly Holman
Lexington Books
D.C. Health and Company; Lexington, Massachusetts; Toronto

AWAKENING YOUR SEXUALITY
A Guide for Recovering Women
by Stephanie Covington, Ph.D.
HarperCollins Publishers, 10 East 53rd Street,
New York, N.Y. USA 10022

THE RECLAIMING OF POWER
by Harvey Jackins
Rational Island Publishers,
P.O. Box 2081, Main Office Station,
Seattle, Washington USA 98111

THE POWER WITHIN PEOPLE
A Community Organizing Perspective 1986.
Authors: Robert A. Antone, Diane L. Hill, Brian A. Myers
Printed by Ball Media, Brantford, ON
Distributed by www.goodminds.com
www.dianehill.net for e-book copy

NUTRITION – Concepts and Controversies
by Eva May Hamilton Eleanor Whitney
West Publishing Co.,
50 West Kellogg Boulevard,
P.O. Box 3526,
St. Paul, Minnesota, USA 55165

I have read many books on recovery – personally and professionally. I recommend that you trust your gut feelings when you are looking for something to read for your healing. It is said "when the student is ready - the teacher will appear." This is a partial list of books that I have read pertaining to Adult Children of Alcoholics, Co-dependence and recovery. There are now even more books on healing and wellness.

RECOMMENDED READINGS

The Magic Within, Mary Lee Zawadski
Double Duty, Claudia Black
All Books by Jane Middleton-Moz
Finding Balance, Kellogg/Harrison
Learning to Love Yourself *and other books* by Sharon Wegscheider-Cruse
Food Addiction, Kay Sheppard
All books written by the pioneers of the National Association of Adult
  Children of Alcoholics with Sharon Wegscheider-Cruse as chairman.
Courage to Heal by Bass/Davis

One of the best websites that I've seen pertaining to Co-dependence
  is called Joy2MeU.com

After many years I started to write again. There are number of books that I
  highly recommend on writing and especially writing to heal the wounds.
Writing the Mind Alive *Linda,* Trichter Metcalf, Ph.D. and Tobin
  Simon, Ph.D.
Writing Alone and with Others Pat Schneider
How the Light Gets In writing as spiritual practice Pat Schneider
Opening it Up by Writing It Down, James W. Pennebaker, Ph.D.
  Joshua M. Smyth, Ph.D.

<u>Writing As a Way of Healing</u>, Louise DeSalvo
<u>Heal Your Self with Writing</u>, Catherine Ann Jones
<u>Writing Your Way Creating a Personal Journal</u>, Ellen Jaffe

ABOUT THE AUTHOR

Barbara-Helen Hill is from Six Nations, Grand River Territory, located in Southern Ontario. She is a graduate of the En'owkin International School of Writing. She has a BA in Native American Aesthetics, Creative Narrative and a Masters in American Studies.

Barbara-Helen is a retired counsellor. She is now off on another adventure in the art world where she is a self-taught Fibre Artist. Her quilted wall hangings and Art Dolls live in different parts of the world and she is now trying her hand at other art forms. In addition to being a fibre artist, she is also a published author. Her poetry, short stories, and essays can be found in many anthologies both in Canada and the United States.

She encourages all people to look for their roots, their history, and to write their own stories. We can tell our stories and show that we are still here.

11069319R00115

Made in the USA
San Bernardino, CA
03 December 2018